HDInsight Essentials

Second Edition

Learn how to build and deploy a modern big data
architecture to empower your business

Rajesh Nadipalli

BIRMINGHAM - MUMBAI

HDInsight Essentials

Second Edition

First published: September 2013

Second edition: January 2015

Production reference: 1200115

Published by Packt Publishing Ltd.
Livery Place
35 Livery Street
Birmingham B3 2PB, UK.

ISBN 978-1-78439-942-9

www.packtpub.com

Credits

Author
Rajesh Nadipalli

Reviewers
Simon Elliston Ball

Anindita Basak

Rami Vemula

Commissioning Editor
Taron Pereira

Acquisition Editor
Owen Roberts

Content Development Editor
Rohit Kumar Singh

Technical Editors
Madhuri Das

Taabish Khan

Copy Editor
Rashmi Sawant

Project Coordinator
Mary Alex

Proofreaders
Ting Baker

Ameesha Green

Indexer
Rekha Nair

Production Coordinator
Melwyn D'sa

Cover Work
Melwyn D'sa

About the Author

Rajesh Nadipalli currently manages software architecture and delivery of Zaloni's Bedrock Data Management Platform, which enables customers to quickly and easily realize true Hadoop-based Enterprise Data Lakes. Rajesh is also an instructor and a content provider for Hadoop training, including Hadoop development, Hive, Pig, and HBase. In his previous role as a senior solutions architect, he evaluated big data goals for his clients, recommended a target state architecture, and conducted proof of concepts and production implementation. His clients include Verizon, American Express, NetApp, Cisco, EMC, and UnitedHealth Group.

Prior to Zaloni, Rajesh worked for Cisco Systems for 12 years and held a technical leadership position. His key focus areas have been data management, enterprise architecture, business intelligence, data warehousing, and Extract Transform Load (ETL). He has demonstrated success by delivering scalable data management and BI solutions that empower business to make informed decisions.

Rajesh authored the first version of the book *HDInsight Essentials*, *Packt Publishing*, released in September 2013, the first book in print for HDInsight, providing data architects, developers, and managers with an introduction to the new Hadoop distribution from Microsoft.

He has over 18 years of IT experience. He holds an MBA from North Carolina State University and a BSc degree in Electronics and Electrical from the University of Mumbai, India.

I would like to thank my family for their unconditional love, support, and patience during the entire process.

To my friends and coworkers at Zaloni, thank you for inspiring and encouraging me.

And finally a shout-out to all the folks at Packt Publishing for being really professional.

About the Reviewers

Simon Elliston Ball is a solutions engineer at Hortonworks, where he helps a wide range of companies get the best out of Hadoop. Before that, he was the head of big data at Red Gate, creating tools to make HDInsight and Hadoop easier to work with. He has also spoken extensively on big data and NoSQL at conferences around the world.

Anindita Basak works as a big data cloud consultant and a big data Hadoop trainer and is highly enthusiastic about Microsoft Azure and HDInsight along with Hadoop open source ecosystem. She works as a specialist for Fortune 500 brands including cloud and big data based companies in the US. She has been playing with Hadoop on Azure since the incubation phase (`http://www.hadooponazure.com`). Previously, she worked as a module lead for the Alten group and as a senior system analyst at Sonata Software Limited, India, in the Azure Professional Direct Delivery group of Microsoft. She worked as a senior software engineer on implementation and migration of various enterprise applications on the Azure cloud in healthcare, retail, and financial domains. She started her journey with Microsoft Azure in the Microsoft Cloud Integration Engineering (CIE) team and worked as a support engineer in Microsoft India (R&D) Pvt. Ltd.

With more than 6 years of experience in the Microsoft .NET technology stack, she is solely focused on big data cloud and data science. As a Most Valued Blogger, she loves to share her technical experience and expertise through her blog at `http://anindita9.wordpress.com` and `http://anindita9.azurewebsites.net`. You can find more about her on her LinkedIn page and you can follow her at `@imcuteani` on Twitter.

She recently worked as a technical reviewer for the books *HDInsight Essentials* and *Microsoft Tabular Modeling Cookbook*, both by Packt Publishing. She is currently working on *Hadoop Essentials*, also by Packt Publishing.

I would like to thank my mom and dad, Anjana and Ajit Basak, and my affectionate brother, Aditya. Without their support, I could not have reached my goal.

Rami Vemula is a technology consultant who loves to provide scalable software solutions for complex business problems through modern day web technologies and cloud infrastructure. His primary focus is on Microsoft technologies, which include ASP.Net MVC/WebAPI, jQuery, C#, SQL Server, and Azure. He currently works for a reputed multinational consulting firm as a consultant, where he leads and supports a team of talented developers. As a part of his work, he architects, develops, and maintains technical solutions to various clients with Microsoft technologies. He is also a Microsoft Certified ASP.Net and Azure Developer.

He has been a Microsoft MVP since 2011 and an active trainer. He conducts online training on Microsoft web stack technologies. In his free time, he enjoys exploring different technical questions at `http://forums.asp.net` and StackOverflow, and then contributes with prospective solutions through custom written code snippets. He loves to share his technical experience and expertise through his blog at `http://intstrings.com/ramivemula`.

He holds a Master's Degree in Electrical Engineering from California State University, Long Beach, USA. He is married and lives with this wife and parents in Hyderabad, India.

I would like to thank my parents, Ramanaiah and RajaKumari; my wife, Sneha; and the rest of my family and friends for their patience and support throughout my life and helping me achieve all the wonderful milestones and accomplishments. Their consistent encouragement and guidance gave me the strength to overcome all the hurdles and kept me moving forward.

www.PacktPub.com

Support files, eBooks, discount offers, and more

For support files and downloads related to your book, please visit www.PacktPub.com.

Did you know that Packt offers eBook versions of every book published, with PDF and ePub files available? You can upgrade to the eBook version at www.PacktPub.com and as a print book customer, you are entitled to a discount on the eBook copy. Get in touch with us at service@packtpub.com for more details.

At www.PacktPub.com, you can also read a collection of free technical articles, sign up for a range of free newsletters and receive exclusive discounts and offers on Packt books and eBooks.

https://www2.packtpub.com/books/subscription/packtlib

Do you need instant solutions to your IT questions? PacktLib is Packt's online digital book library. Here, you can search, access, and read Packt's entire library of books.

Why subscribe?

- Fully searchable across every book published by Packt
- Copy and paste, print, and bookmark content
- On demand and accessible via a web browser

Free access for Packt account holders

If you have an account with Packt at www.PacktPub.com, you can use this to access PacktLib today and view 9 entirely free books. Simply use your login credentials for immediate access.

Instant updates on new Packt books

Get notified! Find out when new books are published by following @PacktEnterprise on Twitter or the *Packt Enterprise* Facebook page.

Table of Contents

Preface

We live in a connected digital era and we are witnessing unprecedented growth of data. Organizations that are able to analyze big data are demonstrating significant return on investment by detecting fraud, improved operations, and reduced time to analyze with a scale-out architecture such as Hadoop. Azure HDInsight is an enterprise-ready distribution of Hadoop hosted in the cloud and provides advanced integration with Excel and .NET without the need to buy or maintain physical hardware.

This book is your guide to building a modern data architecture using HDInsight to enable your organization to gain insights from various sources, including smart-connected devices, databases, and social media. This book will take you through a journey of building the next generation Enterprise Data Lake that consists of ingestion, transformation, and analysis of big data with a specific use case that can apply to almost any organization.

This book has working code that developers can leverage and extend in order to fit their use cases with additional references for self-learning.

What this book covers

Chapter 1, *Hadoop and HDInsight in a Heartbeat*, covers the business value and the reason behind the big data hype. It provides a primer on Apache Hadoop, core concepts with HDFS, YARN, and the Hadoop 2.*x* ecosystem. Next, it discusses the Microsoft HDInsight platform, its key benefits, and deployment options.

Chapter 2, *Enterprise Data Lake using HDInsight*, covers the main points of the current Enterprise Data Warehouse and provides a path for an enterprise Data Lake based on the Hadoop platform. Additionally, it explains a use case built on the Azure HDInsight service.

Chapter 3, HDInsight Service on Azure, walks you through the steps for provisioning Azure HDInsight. Next, it explains how to explore, monitor, and delete the cluster using the Azure management portal. Next, it provides tools for developers to verify the cluster using a sample program and develop it using HDInsight Emulator.

Chapter 4, Administering Your HDInsight Cluster, covers steps to administer the HDInsight cluster using remote desktop connection to the head node of the cluster. It includes management of Azure Blob storage and introduces you to the Azure scripting environment known as Azure PowerShell.

Chapter 5, Ingest and Organize Data Lake, introduces you to an end-to-end Data Lake solution with a near real life size project and then focuses on various options to ingest data to a HDInsight cluster, including HDFS commands, Azure PowerShell, CloudExplorer, and Sqoop. Next, it provides details on how to organize data using Apache HCatalog. This chapter uses a real life size sample airline project to explain the various concepts.

Chapter 6, Transform Data in the Data Lake, provides you with various options to transform data, including MapReduce, Hive, and Pig. Additionally, it discusses Oozie and Spark, which are also commonly used for transformation. Throughout the chapter, you will be guided with a detailed code for the sample airline project.

Chapter 7, Analyze and Report from Data Lake, provides you with details on how to access and analyze data from the sample airline project using Excel Hive ODBC driver, Excel Power Query, Powerpivot, and PowerMap. Additionally, it discusses RHadoop, Giraph, and Mahout as alternatives to analyze data in the cluster.

Chapter 8, HDInsight 3.1 New Features, provides you with new features that are added to the evolving HDInsight platform with sample use cases for HBase, Tez, and Storm.

Chapter 9, Strategy for a Successful Data Lake Implementation, covers the key challenges for building a production Data Lake and provides guidance on the success path for a sustainable Data Lake. This chapter provides recommendations on architecture, organization, and links to online resources.

What you need for this book

For this book, the following are the prerequisites:

- To build an HDInsight cluster using the Azure cloud service, you will need an Azure account and a laptop with Windows Remote Desktop software to connect to the cluster

- For Excel-based exercises, you will need Office 2013/Excel 2013/Office 365 ProPlus/Office 2010 Professional Plus

- For HDInsight Emulator, which is suited for local development, you will need a Windows laptop with one of these operating systems: Windows 7 Service Pack 1/Windows Server 2008 R2 Service Pack 1/Windows 8/ Windows Server 2012.

Who this book is for

This book is designed for data architects, developers, managers, and business users who want to modernize their data architectures leveraging the HDInsight distribution of Hadoop. It guides you through the business values of big data, the main points of current EDW (Enterprise Data Warehouse), steps for building the next generation Data Lake, and development tools with real life examples.

The book explains the journey to a Data Lake with a modular approach for ingesting, transforming, and reporting on a Data Lake leveraging HDInsight platform and Excel for powerful analysis and reporting.

Conventions

In this book, you will find a number of text styles that distinguish between different kinds of information. Here are some examples of these styles and an explanation of their meaning.

Code words in text, database table names, folder names, filenames, file extensions, pathnames, dummy URLs, user input, and Twitter handles are shown as follows: "I have selected hdind and the complete URL is `hdind.azurehdinsight.net`."

Any command-line input or output is written as follows:

```
# Import PublishSettingsFile that was saved from last step
Import-AzurePublishSettingsFile "C:\Users\Administrator\Downloads\Pay-As-You-Go-Free Trial-11-21-2014-credentials.publishsettings"
```

New terms and **important words** are shown in bold. Words that you see on the screen, for example, in menus or dialog boxes, appear in the text like this: "You can select the desired configuration **Two Head Nodes on an Extra Large (A4) instance included** or **Two Head Nodes on a Large (A3) instance included**."

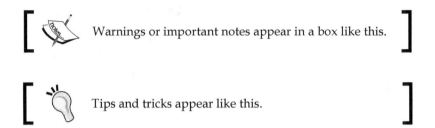

Warnings or important notes appear in a box like this.

Tips and tricks appear like this.

Reader feedback

Feedback from our readers is always welcome. Let us know what you think about this book—what you liked or disliked. Reader feedback is important for us as it helps us develop titles that you will really get the most out of.

To send us general feedback, simply e-mail feedback@packtpub.com, and mention the book's title in the subject of your message.

If there is a topic that you have expertise in and you are interested in either writing or contributing to a book, see our author guide at www.packtpub.com/authors.

Customer support

Now that you are the proud owner of a Packt book, we have a number of things to help you to get the most from your purchase.

Downloading the example code

You can download the example code files from your account at http://www.packtpub.com for all the Packt Publishing books you have purchased. If you purchased this book elsewhere, you can visit http://www.packtpub.com/support and register to have the files e-mailed directly to you.

Errata

Although we have taken every care to ensure the accuracy of our content, mistakes do happen. If you find a mistake in one of our books—maybe a mistake in the text or the code—we would be grateful if you could report this to us. By doing so, you can save other readers from frustration and help us improve subsequent versions of this book. If you find any errata, please report them by visiting http://www.packtpub.com/submit-errata, selecting your book, clicking on the **Errata Submission Form** link, and entering the details of your errata.

Once your errata are verified, your submission will be accepted and the errata will be uploaded to our website or added to any list of existing errata under the Errata section of that title.

To view the previously submitted errata, go to https://www.packtpub.com/books/content/support and enter the name of the book in the search field. The required information will appear under the **Errata** section.

Piracy

Piracy of copyrighted material on the Internet is an ongoing problem across all media. At Packt, we take the protection of our copyright and licenses very seriously. If you come across any illegal copies of our works in any form on the Internet, please provide us with the location address or website name immediately so that we can pursue a remedy.

Please contact us at copyright@packtpub.com with a link to the suspected pirated material.

We appreciate your help in protecting our authors and our ability to bring you valuable content.

Questions

If you have a problem with any aspect of this book, you can contact us at questions@packtpub.com, and we will do our best to address the problem.

1
Hadoop and HDInsight in a Heartbeat

This chapter will provide an overview of Apache Hadoop and Microsoft big data strategy, where Microsoft HDInsight plays an important role. We will cover the following topics:

- The era of big data
- Hadoop concepts
- Hadoop distributions
- HDInsight overview
- Hadoop on Windows deployment options

Data is everywhere

We live in a digital era and are always connected with friends and family using social media and smartphones. In 2014, every second over 5,700 tweets were sent and 800 links were shared using Facebook and the digital universe was about 1.7 MB per minute for every person on Earth (source: IDC 2014 report). This amount of data sharing and storing is unprecedented and is contributing to what is known as **big data**.

The following infographic shows you the details of our current use of the top social media sites (source `https://leveragenewagemedia.com/`):

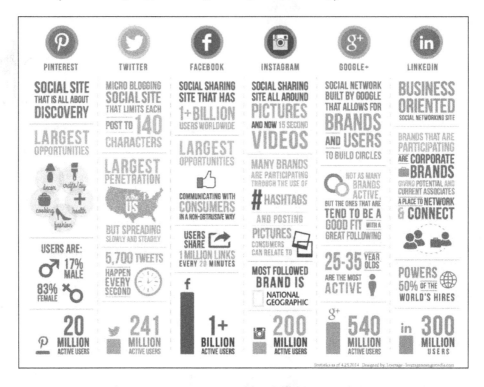

Other contributors to big data are the smart connected devices such as smartphones, appliances, cars, sensors, and pretty much everything that we use today and is connected to the Internet. These devices, which will soon be in trillions, continuously collect data and communicate with each other about their environment to make intelligent decisions and help us live better. This digitization of the world has added to the exponential growth of big data.

The following figure depicts the trend analysis done by Microsoft Azure, which shows the evolution of big data "internet of things". In the period 1980 to 1990, IT systems ERM/CRM primarily generated data in a well-structured format with volume in GBs. In the period between 1990 and 2000, the Web and mobile applications emerged and now the data volumes increased to terabytes. After the year 2000, social networking sites, Wikis, blogs, and smart devices emerged and now we are dealing with petabytes of data. The section in blue highlights the big data era that includes social media, sensors, and images where **Volume**, **Velocity**, and **Variety** are the norms. One related key trend is the price of hardware, which dropped from $190/GB in 1980 to $0.07/GB in 2010. This has been a key enabler in big data adoption.

According to the 2014 IDC digital universe report, the growth trend will continue and double in size every two years. In 2013, about 4.4 zettabytes were created and in 2020 the forecast is 44 zettabytes, which is 44 trillion gigabytes (source: `http://www.emc.com/leadership/digital-universe/2014iview/executive-summary.htm`).

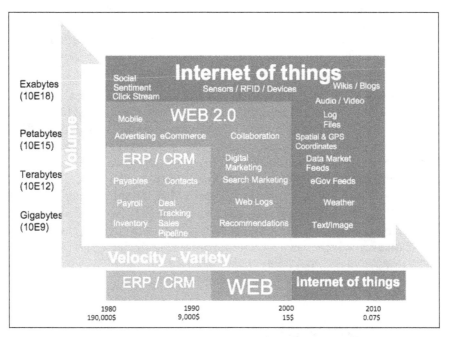

Source: Microsoft TechEd North America 2014 From Zero to Data Insights from HDInsight on Microsoft Azure

Business value of big data

While we generated 4.4 zettabytes of data in 2013, *only five percent* of it was actually analyzed and this is the real opportunity of big data. The IDC report forecasts that by 2020, we will analyze over 35 percent of generated data by making smarter sensors and devices. This data will drive new consumer and business behavior that will drive trillions of dollars in opportunity for IT vendors and organizations analyzing this data.

Let's look at some real use cases that have benefited from Big Data:

- IT systems in all major banks are constantly monitoring fraudulent activities and alerting customers within milliseconds. These systems apply complex business rules and analyze historical data, geography, type of vendor, and other parameters based on the customer to get accurate results.

- Commercial drones are transforming agriculture by analyzing real-time aerial images and identifying the problem areas. These drones are cheaper and more efficient than satellite imagery, as they fly under the clouds and can take images anytime. They identify irrigation issues related to water, pests, or fungal infections, which thereby, increases the crop productivity and quality. These drones are equipped with technology to capture high quality images every second and transfer them to a cloud hosted big data system for further processing. (You can refer to `http://www.technologyreview.com/featuredstory/526491/agricultural-drones/`.)

- Developers of the blockbuster *Halo 4* game were tasked to analyze player preferences and support an online tournament in the cloud. The game attracted over 4 million players in its first five days after the launch. The development team had to also design a solution that kept track of leader board for the global *Halo 4 Infinity Challenge*, which was open to all players. The development team chose the Azure HDInsight service to analyze the massive amounts of unstructured data in a distributed manner. The results from HDInsight were reported using Microsoft SQL Server PowerPivot and Sharepoint, and business was extremely happy with the response times for their queries, which was a few hours, or less (source: `http://www.microsoft.com/casestudies/Windows-Azure/343-Industries/343-Industries-Gets-New-User-Insights-from-Big-Data-in-the-Cloud/710000002102`).

Hadoop concepts

Apache Hadoop is the leading open source big data platform that can store and analyze massive amounts of structured and unstructured data efficiently and can be hosted on low cost commodity hardware. There are other technologies that complement Hadoop under the big data umbrella such as MongoDB, a NoSQL database; Cassandra, a document database; and VoltDB, an in-memory database. This section describes Apache Hadoop core concepts and its ecosystem.

Brief history of Hadoop

Doug Cutting created Hadoop; he named it after his kid's stuffed yellow elephant and it has no real meaning. In 2004, the initial version of Hadoop was launched as **Nutch Distributed Filesystem (NDFS)**. In February 2006, Apache Hadoop project was officially started as a standalone development for MapReduce and HDFS. By 2008, Yahoo adopted Hadoop as the engine of its Web search with a cluster size of around 10,000. In the same year, 2008, Hadoop graduated at top-level Apache project confirming its success. In 2012, Hadoop 2.*x* was launched with YARN, enabling Hadoop to take on various types of workloads.

Today, Hadoop is known by just about every IT architect and business executive as the open source big data platform and is used across all industries and sizes of organizations.

Core components

In this section, we will explore what Hadoop actually comprises. At the basic-level, Hadoop consists of the following four layers:

- **Hadoop Common**: A set of common libraries and utilities used by Hadoop modules.

- **Hadoop Distributed File System** (**HDFS**): A scalable and fault tolerant distributed filesystem to data in any form. HDFS can be installed on commodity hardware and replicates the data three times (which is configurable) to make the filesystem robust and tolerate partial hardware failures.

- **Yet Another Resource Negotiator** (**YARN**): From Hadoop 2.0, YARN is the cluster management layer to handle various workloads on the cluster.

- **MapReduce**: MapReduce is a framework that allows parallel processing of data in Hadoop. It breaks a job into smaller tasks and distributes the load to servers that have the relevant data. The framework effectively executes tasks on nodes where data is present thereby reducing the network and disk I/O required to move data.

The following figure shows you the high-level Hadoop 2.0 core components:

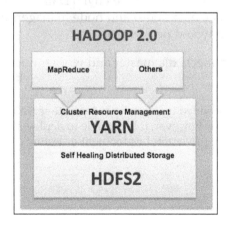

The preceding figure shows you the components that form the basic Hadoop framework. In past few years, a vast array of new components have emerged in the Hadoop ecosystem that take advantage of YARN making Hadoop faster, better, and suitable for various types of workloads. The following figure shows you the Hadoop framework with these new components:

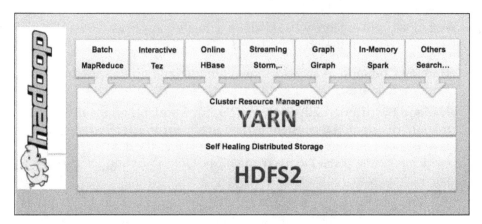

Hadoop cluster layout

Each Hadoop cluster has the following two types of machines:

- **Master nodes**: These consist of the HDFS NameNode, HDFS Secondary NameNode, and YARN ResourceManager.
- **Worker nodes**: These consist of the HDFS DataNodes and YARN NodeManagers. The data nodes and node managers are collocated for optimal data locality and performance.

A network switch interconnects the master and worker nodes.

 It is recommended that you have separate servers for each of the master nodes; however, it is possible to deploy all the master nodes onto a single server for development or testing environments.

The following figure shows you the typical Hadoop cluster layout:

Let's review the key functions of the master and worker nodes:

- **NameNode**: This is the master for the distributed filesystem and maintains metadata. This metadata has the listing of all the files and the location of each block of a file, which are stored across the various slaves. Without a NameNode, HDFS is not accessible. From Hadoop 2.0 onwards, NameNode **HA (High Availability)** can be configured with active and standby servers.

- **Secondary NameNode**: This is an assistant to NameNode. It communicates only with NameNode to take snapshots of HDFS metadata at intervals that is configured at cluster level.

- **YARN ResourceManager**: This server is a scheduler that allocates available resources in the cluster among the competing applications.

- **Worker nodes**: The Hadoop cluster will have several worker nodes that handle two types of functions: HDFS DataNode and YARN NodeManager. It is typical that each worker node handles both these functions for optimal data locality. This means that processing happens on the data that is local to the node and follows the principle "move code and not data".

HDFS overview

This section will look into the distributed filesystem in detail. The following figure shows you a Hadoop cluster with four data nodes and NameNode in HA mode. The NameNode is the bookkeeper for HDFS and keeps track of the following details:

- List of all files in HDFS
- Blocks associated with each file
- Location of each block including the replicated blocks

Starting with HDFS 2.0, NameNode is no longer a single point of failure that eliminates any business impact in case of hardware failures.

 Secondary NameNode is not required in NameNode HA configuration, as the Standby NameNode performs the tasks of the Secondary NameNode.

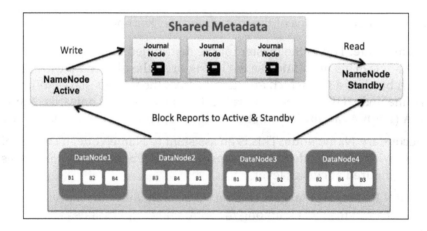

Next, let's review how data is written and read from HDFS.

Writing a file to HDFS

When a file is ingested to Hadoop, it is first divided into several blocks where each block is typically 64 MB in size that can be configured by administrators. Next, each block is replicated three times onto different data nodes for business continuity so that even if one data node goes down, the replicas come to the rescue. The replication factor is configurable and can be increased or decreased as desired. The preceding figure shows you an example of a file called `MyBigfile.txt` that is split into four blocks **B1**, **B2**, **B3**, and **B4**. Each block is replicated three times across different data nodes.

The active NameNode is responsible for all client operations and writes information about the new file and blocks the shared metadata and the standby NameNode reads from this shared metadata. The shared metadata requires a group of daemons called **journal nodes**.

Reading a file from HDFS

When a request to read a file is made, the active NameNode refers to the shared metadata in order to identify the blocks associated with the file and the locations of those blocks. In our example, the large file, `MyBigfile.txt`, the NameNode will return a location for each of the four blocks B1, B2, B3, and B4. If a particular data node is down, then the nearest and not so busy replica's block is loaded.

HDFS basic commands

Let's look at the commonly used Hadoop commands used to access the distributed filesystem:

Command	Syntax
Listing of files in a directory	`hadoop fs -ls /user`
Create a new directory	`hadoop fs -mkdir /user/guest/newdirectory`
Copy a file from a local machine to Hadoop	`hadoop fs -put C:\Users\Administrator\ Downloads\localfile.csv /user/rajn/ newdirectory/hadoopfile.txt`
Copy a file from Hadoop to a local machine	`hadoop fs -get /user/rajn/newdirectory/ hadoopfile.txt C:\Users\Administrator\Desktop\`
Tail last few lines of a large file in Hadoop	`hadoop fs -tail /user/rajn/newdirectory/ hadoopfile.txt`
View the complete contents of a file in Hadoop	`hadoop fs -cat /user/rajn/newdirectory/ hadoopfile.txt`
Remove a complete directory from Hadoop	`hadoop fs -rm -r /user/rajn/newdirectory`
Check the Hadoop filesystem space utilization	`hadoop fs -du /`

For a complete list of Hadoop commands, refer to the link `http://hadoop.apache.org/docs/current/hadoop-project-dist/hadoop-common/FileSystemShell.html`.

YARN overview

Now that we are able to save the large file, the next obvious need would be to process this file and get something useful out of it such as a summary report. Hadoop **YARN**, which stands for **Yet Another Resource Manager**, is designed for distributed data processing and is the architectural center of Hadoop. This area in Hadoop has gone through a major rearchitecturing in Version 2.0 of Hadoop and YARN has enabled Hadoop to be a true multiuse data platform that can handle batch processing, real-time streaming, interactive SQL, and is extensible for other custom engines. YARN is flexible, efficient, provides resource sharing, and is fault-tolerant.

YARN consists of a central ResourceManager that arbitrates all available cluster resources and per-node NodeManagers that take directions from the ResourceManager and are responsible for managing resources available on a single node. NodeManagers have containers that perform the real computation.

ResourceManager has the following main components:

- **Scheduler**: This is responsible for allocating resources to various running applications, subject to constraints of capacities and queues that are configured

- **Applications Manager**: This is responsible for accepting job submissions, negotiating the first container for executing the application, which is called "Application Master"

NodeManager is the worker bee and is responsible for managing containers, monitoring their resource usage (CPU, memory, disk, and network), and reporting the same to the ResourceManager. The two types of containers present are as follows:

- **Application Master**: This is one per application and has the responsibility of negotiating with appropriate resource containers from the ResourceManager, tracking their status, and monitoring their progress.

- **Application Containers**: This gets launched as per the application specifications. An example of an application is MapReduce, which is used for batch processing.

YARN application life cycle

Let's understand how the various components in YARN actually interact with a walkthrough of an application lifecycle. The following figure shows you a Hadoop cluster with one master ResourceManager and four worker NodeManagers:

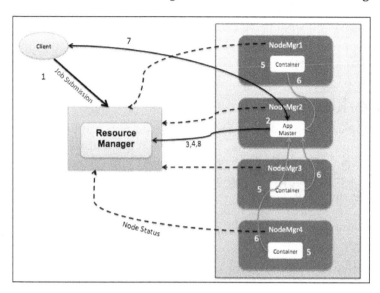

Let's walkthrough the sequence of events in a life of an application such as MapReduce job:

1. The client program submits an application request to the ResourceManager and provides the necessary specifications to launch the application.

2. The ResourceManager takes over the responsibility to identify a container to be started as an Application Master and then launches the Application Master, which in our case is NodeManager 2 (**NodeMgr2**).

3. The Application Master on boot-up registers with the ResourceManager. This allows the client program to get visibility on which Node is handling the Application Master for further communication.

4. The Application Master negotiates with the ResourceManager for containers to perform the actual tasks. In the preceding figure, the application master requested three resource containers.

5. On successful container allocations, the Application Master launches the container by providing the specifications to the NodeManager.

6. The application code executing within the container provides status and progress information to the Application Master.

7. During the application execution, the client who submits the program communicates directly with the Application Master to get status, progress, and updates.

8. After the application is complete, the Application Master deregisters with the ResourceManager and shuts down, allowing all the containers associated with that application to be repurposed.

YARN workloads

Prior to Hadoop 2.0, MapReduce was the standard approach to process data on Hadoop. With the introduction of YARN, which has a flexible architecture, various other types of workload are now supported and are now great alternatives to MapReduce with better performance and management. Here is a list of commonly used workloads on top of YARN:

- **Batch**: MapReduce that is the compatible with Hadoop 1.*x*
- **Script**: Pig
- **Interactive SQL**: Hive or Tez
- **NoSQL**: HBase and Accumulo
- **Streaming**: Storm
- **In-memory**: Spark
- **Search**: SOLR

The combination of HDFS, which is a distributed data store, and YARN, which is a flexible data operating system, make Hadoop a true multiuse data platform enabling modern data architecture.

Hadoop distributions

Apache Hadoop is an open source software, and is repackaged and distributed by vendors who offer enterprise support and additional applications to manage Hadoop. The following is the listing of popular commercial distributions:

- Amazon Elastic MapReduce (http://aws.amazon.com/ elasticmapreduce/)
- Cloudera (http://www.cloudera.com/content/cloudera/en/home.html)
- EMC PivotalHD (http://gopivotal.com/)

- Hortonworks HDP (http://hortonworks.com/)
- IBM BigInsights (http://www-01.ibm.com/software/data/infosphere/biginsights/)
- MapR (http://mapr.com/)
- Microsoft HDInsight (cloud: http://azure.microsoft.com/en-us/services/hdinsight/)

HDInsight overview

HDInsight is an enterprise-ready distribution of Hadoop that runs on Windows servers and on Azure HDInsight cloud service (PaaS). It is a 100 percent Apache Hadoop-based service in the cloud. HDInsight was developed in partnership with Hortonworks and Microsoft. Enterprises can now harness the power of Hadoop on Windows servers and Windows Azure cloud service.

The following are the key differentiators for HDInsight distribution:

- **Enterprise-ready Hadoop**: HDInsight is backed by Microsoft support, and runs on standard Windows servers. IT teams can leverage Hadoop with the **Platform as a Service** (**PaaS**) reducing the operations overhead.
- **Analytics using Excel**: With Excel integration, your business users can visualize and analyze Hadoop data in compelling new ways with an easy to use familiar tool. The Excel add-ons PowerBI, PowerPivot, PowerQuery, and PowerMap integrate with HDInsight.
- **Develop in your favorite language**: HDInsight has powerful programming extensions for languages, including .NET, C#, Java, and more.
- **Scale using cloud offering**: Azure HDInsight service enables customers to scale quickly as per the project needs and have a seamless interface between HDFS and Azure Blob storage.
- **Connect on-premises Hadoop cluster with the cloud**: With HDInsight, you can move Hadoop data from an on-site data center to the Azure cloud for backup, dev/test, and cloud bursting scenarios.
- **Includes NoSQL transactional capabilities**: HDInsight also includes Apache HBase, a columnar NoSQL database that runs on top of Hadoop and allows large **online transactional processing** (**OLTP**).
- **HDInsight Emulator**: The HDInsight Emulator provides a local development environment for Azure HDInsight without the need for a cloud subscription. This can be installed using the Microsoft Web Platform installer.

HDInsight and Hadoop relationship

HDInsight is an Apache Hadoop-based service. Let's review the stack in detail. The following figure shows you the stacks that make HDInsight:

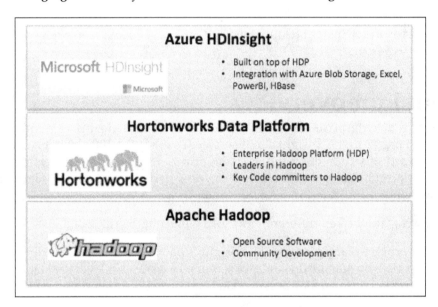

The various components are as follows:

- **Apache Hadoop**: This is an open source software that allows distributed storage and computation. Hadoop is reliable and scalable.

- **Hortonworks Data Platform** (**HDP**): This is an open source Apache Hadoop data platform, architected for the enterprise on Linux and Windows servers. It has a comprehensive set of capabilities aligned to the following functional areas: data management, data access, data governance, security, and operations. The following are the key **Apache Software Foundation** (**ASF**) projects have been led and are included in HDP:

    - **Apache Falcon**: Falcon is a framework used for simplifying data management and pipeline processing in Hadoop. It also enables disaster recovery and data retention use cases.

    - **Apache Tez**: Tez is an extensible framework used for building YARN-based, high performance batch, and interactive data processing applications in Hadoop. Projects such as Hive and Pig can leverage Tez and get an improved performance.

- ◦ **Apache Knox**: Knox is a system that provides a single point of authentication and access for Hadoop services in a cluster.

- ◦ **Apache Ambari**: Ambari is an operational framework used for provisioning; managing, and monitoring Apache Hadoop clusters.

- **Azure HDInsight**: This has been built in partnership with Hortonworks on top of HDP for Microsoft Servers and Azure cloud service. It has the following key additional value added services provided by Microsoft:

  - ◦ Integration with Azure Blob storage Excel, PowerBI, SQL Server, .Net, C#, Java, and others

  - ◦ Azure PowerShell, which is a powerful scripting environment that can be used to control, automate, and develop workloads in HDInsight

Hadoop on Windows deployment options

Apache Hadoop can be deployed on Windows either on physical servers or in the cloud. This section reviews the various options for Hadoop on Windows.

Microsoft Azure HDInsight Service

Microsoft Azure is a cloud solution that allows one to rent, compute, and store resources on-demand for the duration of a project. HDInsight is a service that utilizes these elastic services and allows us to quickly create a Hadoop cluster for big data processing. HDInsight cluster is completely integrated with low-cost Blob storage and allows other programs to directly leverage data in Blob storage.

HDInsight Emulator

Microsoft HDInsight Emulator for Azure is a single node Hadoop cluster with key components installed and configured that is great for development, initial prototyping, and promoting code to production cluster.

HDInsight Emulator requires a 64-bit version of Windows and one of the following operating systems will suffice: Windows 7 Service Pack 1, Windows Server 2008 R2 Service Pack1, Windows 8, or Windows Server 2012.

Hortonworks Data Platform (HDP) for Windows

HDP for Windows can be deployed on multiple servers. With this option, you have complete control over the servers and can scale as per your project needs in your own data center. This option, however, does not have the additional value added features provided by HDInsight.

HDP 2.2 requires a 64-bit version of Windows Server 2008 or Windows Server 2012.

Summary

We live in a connected digital era and are witnessing unprecedented growth of data. Organizations that are able to analyze Big Data are demonstrating significant return on investment by detecting fraud, improved operations, and reduced time to analyze a scale-out architecture. Apache Hadoop is the leading open source big data platform with strong and diverse ecosystem projects that enable organizations to build a modern data architecture. At the core, Hadoop has two key components—Hadoop Distributed File System also known as HDFS and a cluster resource manager known as YARN. YARN has enabled Hadoop to be a true multiuse data platform that can handle batch processing, real-time streaming, interactive SQL, and others.

Microsoft HDInsight is an enterprise-ready distribution of Hadoop on the cloud that has been developed in partnership with Hortonworks and Microsoft. Key benefits of HDInsight include: scale up/down as required, analysis using Excel, connect on-premise Hadoop cluster with the cloud, and flexible programming and support for NoSQL transactional database.

In the next chapter, we will take a look at how to build an Enterprise Data Lake using HDInsight.

2
Enterprise Data Lake using HDInsight

Current IT architecture uses a **Enterprise Data Warehouse** (**EDW**) as the centralized repository that feeds several business data marts to drive business intelligence and data mining systems. With the advent of smart connected devices and social media that generate petabytes of data, these current relational EDWs are not able to scale and meet the business needs. This chapter will discuss how to build a modern data architecture that extends the EDW with the Hadoop ecosystem.

In this chapter, we will cover the following topics:

- Enterprise Data Warehouse architecture
- Next generation Hadoop-based Data Lake architecture
- The journey to your Data Lake dream
- Tools and technology in the Hadoop ecosystem
- Use case powered by Microsoft HDInsight

Enterprise Data Warehouse architecture

Over the last 3 decades, organizations have built EDW that consolidates data from various sources across the organization to enable business decisions, typically, related to current operational metrics and future what-if analysis for strategy decisions.

The following figure shows you a typical EDW architecture and also shows how information flows from the various source systems to the hands of business users:

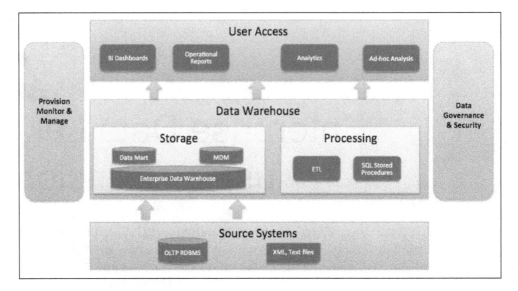

Let's take a look at the stack from bottom to top.

Source systems

Typical data sources for an EDW are as follows:

- **OLTP databases**: These databases store data for transactional systems such as **customer relationship management (CRM)**, **Enterprise resource planning (ERP)**, including manufacturing, inventory, shipping, and others.
- **XML and Text Files**: Data is also received in the form of text files, which are generally delimited, or XML, or some other fixed format known within the organization.

Data warehouse

A data warehouse has two key subcomponents: storage and processing. Let's review these in detail.

Storage

The following are the key data stores for EDW:

- **EDW**: This is the heart of the complete architecture and is a relational database that hosts data from disparate sources in a consistent format such as base facts and dimensions. It is organized by the subject area/domain and preserves history for several years to enable analytics, trends, and ad hoc queries. An EDW infrastructure needs to be robust and scalable to meet the business continuity and growth requirements.

- **Data marts**: Each data mart is a relational database and is a subset of EDW typically, focusing on one subject area such as finance. It queries base facts from EDW and builds summarized facts and stores them as star or snowflake dimensional models.

- **MDM**: **Master data management** or MDM is a relational database that stores reference data to ensure consistent reporting across various business units of an organization. Common MDM datasets include products, customers, and accounts. MDM systems require governance to ensure reporting from various data marts that can be correlated and are consistent.

Processing

The following are the key processing mechanisms for EDW:

- **ETL: Extract, Transform, and Load** is a standard data warehouse design pattern that has three key steps: extract from various sources, transform to cleanse, and convert data to the information that is then loaded to various data marts for reporting. There are several tools in the marketplace such as Microsoft SQL Server Integration Services, Informatica, Pentaho, and others. ETL workflows are scheduled typically at daily frequency to update EDW facts and dimensions.

- **SQL-based stored procedures**: This is an alternative to using ETL tools and transform data natively using database features. Most relational databases provide custom stored procedure capabilities such as SQL Server, Oracle, and IBM.

User access

The following are typically used access mechanisms:

- **BI dashboard**: Business intelligence tools access the data from data marts to provide **key performance indicators (KPI)**, scorecards, and dashboards. They allow the business to look at historical trends, current operational performance, perform what-if analysis, and predict future trends. There are several tools in the marketplace, including Microsoft SQL Server Reporting Services, Microsoft Power BI, Oracle Business Intelligence Enterprise Edition (OBIEE), SAP BusinessObjects, Tableau, and so on.

- **Ad hoc analysis**: IT organizations have realized the need to provide business with direct access to certain data for discovery and ad hoc analysis. Excel and several reporting tools fit this need.

- **Operational reports**: These are the day-to-day canned reports required to run the businesses such as daily sales collections, and customer support tickets opened and closed for the current day. These reports are generally required to be near real time and are based on one source system such as customer help desk system. There are several reporting systems such as SQL Server Reporting Services, IBM Cognos, and others that fit this need.

- **Analytics**: Analytical reports look for trends such as how is my customer satisfaction trending over time and the average operational overhead in dollars for support. These reports typically have a one day/week refresh cycle and collect information from multiple sources such as help desk system and PPM. Business intelligence tools typically fit this need.

Provisioning and monitoring

This area of the architecture is responsible for the following functions:

- Managing deployments of ETL code across various environments: development, test, and production
- Monitoring ingestions and jobs to ensure service-level agreements are met
- Operating procedures to recover in case of a failure

Data governance and security

Effective data governance in an enterprise ensures that data is consistent across departments and requires data stewards that identify and enforce the system of records. This requires tools, processes, and people to have high-quality data.

Security on the enterprise data warehouse affects all layers of the architecture and ensures that the right people have the right access to data. There are several technologies that enable fine-grained access at database level, table level, and row level. The filesystem can be encrypted to provide additional level of security.

Pain points of EDW

Based on an IDC research, by 2020, the digital universe will reach 40 ZB (zettabyte), which is a 50-fold growth from the beginning of 2010. (Reference: `http://www.emc.com/about/news/press/2012/20121211-01.htm`). Current IT data architectures based on EDW were not designed to handle this amount of data and are being stretched. The following are the key pain points of EDW:

- **Scale**: A data warehouse was built to handle data in terabytes (TBs) and currently business needs are reaching petabytes (PB). Typically, data warehouse DBAs archive data older than a certain date window like 5 years to address this issue. This data can be a useful information for long-term trends.

- **Cost**: EDW is typically an appliance-based model with proprietary engineered hardware and software supported by vendors such as Teradata, Oracle, IBM, and others. Upgrades are expensive and typically require all servers to be identical.

- **Unstructured data**: Data warehouses struggle to handle unstructured data such as logfiles, social media, and machine data.

- **Timeliness**: To produce business insights, data has to go through several transformations. Current EDW architectures are unable to meet growth and business demands for new insights on their data.

The next generation Hadoop-based Enterprise data architecture

We will now see how modern data architecture addresses the pain points of a legacy EDW and prepares the organization to handle the big wave of data. It is designed to handle both structured and unstructured data in a cost effective and scalable mode. This provides the business with a wide range of new capabilities and opportunities to gain insights.

Instead of a complete EDW replacement, this architecture leverages the existing investment by preserving end-user interfaces that require relational stores. In this model, Hadoop becomes the prime data store and EDW is used to store aggregates.

The following figure shows you how to transition from legacy EDW-based solutions to a hybrid Hadoop-based ecosystem, where EDW's role is reduced to hosting the aggregated data enabling queries via well-established tools that are relational in nature:

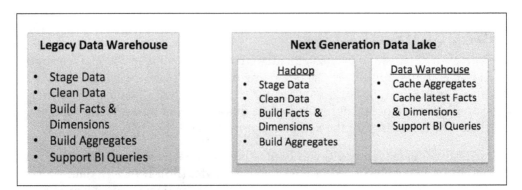

The following figure shows you the new reference architecture for a Hadoop-based Data Lake:

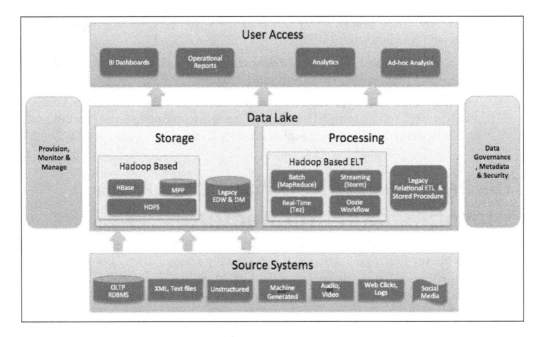

Let's take a look at the stack from bottom to top.

Source systems

The following are the data sources in the next generation architecture:

- **OLTP**: These databases store data for transactional systems such as CRM, ERP, including manufacturing, inventory, shipping, and others
- **XML and text files**: Data is also received in the form of text files, which are generally delimited, or XML, or some other fixed format known within the organization
- **Unstructured**: Information from various websites, word documents, PDF documents, and other forms that don't have fixed structure or semantics
- **Machine-generated data**: Data captured from automated systems such as telemetry is used primarily for monitoring and performance
- **Audio, video, and images**: Audio, video recordings, and images that are difficult to analyze due to their binary formats
- **Web clicks and logs**: Click stream and logs from websites that provide you with valuable information about consumer behavior
- **Social media**: Messages, tweets, and posts on several social media platforms such as Twitter, Facebook, and Google that provide you with consumer sentiments

Data Lake

This is the heart of the architecture that includes storage and compute.

Storage

- The following are the key data stores for a Data Lake:
- **Hadoop HDFS**: HDFS is a core component of Hadoop that provides a data store that can scale as per the business needs and run on any commodity hardware and is 100 percent open source. In this new architecture, all the source data first lands to HDFS and is then processed and exported to other databases or applications.
- **Hadoop HBase**: HBase is a distributed and scalable NoSQL database that provides low latency option on Hadoop. It uses HDFS to store data files and is hosted on Hadoop cluster.

- **Hadoop MPP databases**: MPP stands for massively parallel processing where data can be stored in HDFS and access to MPP can be through SQL or APIs enabling easier integration to existing applications. We are seeing a lot of innovations in this area.

- **Legacy EDW and DM**: This architecture leverages current investment on EDW, DM, and MDM. The size of EDW, however, is reduced as HDFS takes the heavy lifting and only the summary data is hosted in EDW.

Processing

The following are the processing mechanisms for Data Lake:

- **Hadoop Batch (MapReduce)**: MapReduce is a core Hadoop component and is a good fit to replace ETL batch jobs. MapReduce has built-in fault tolerance and runs on the same HDFS data nodes that can scale when the demand increases.

- **Hadoop Streaming (Storm)**: Storm allows the distributed real-time computation system on top of the Hadoop cluster. A good use of this technology is the real-time security alerts on dashboards that require low latency and cannot wait for a complete batch execution.

- **Hadoop Real time (Tez)**: Tez is an extensible framework that allows developers to write native YARN applications that can handle workloads ranging from interactive to batch. Additionally projects such as Hive and Pig can run over Tez and benefit from performance gains over MapReduce.

- **Hadoop Oozie workflows**: This enables creation of workflow jobs to orchestrate Hive, Pig, and MapReduce tasks.

- **Legacy ETL and stored procedures**: This block in the architecture represents the legacy ETL code that will gradually shrink as Hadoop ecosystem builds more capabilities to handle various workloads.

User access

This part of the architecture remains identical to the traditional data warehouse architecture with BI dashboards, operational reports, analytics, and ad hoc queries. This architecture does provide additional capabilities such as fraud detection, predictive analytics, 360 views of customers, and longer duration of history reports.

Provisioning and monitoring

The new architecture will also require provisioning and monitoring capabilities such as the EDW-based architecture that includes managing deployments, monitoring jobs, and operations.

A Data Lake architecture does have additional components from the Hadoop stack that add to the complexity and we need new tools that typically come with the Hadoop distribution such as Ambari.

Data governance, security, and metadata

Data governance process and tools are built for EDW-based architecture that can be extended to the Data Lake base architecture.

Current tools for security on Hadoop-based Data Lake are not sophisticated but will improve in the next few years as adoption of Hadoop is gaining steam.

The core of Hadoop is essentially a filesystem whose management requires metadata for organizing, transforming, and publishing information from these files. This requires a new metadata component for the Data Lake architecture. Apache HCatalog does have some basic metadata capabilities but needs to be extended to capture operational and business-level metadata.

Journey to your Data Lake dream

Hadoop's HDFS and YARN are the core components for the next generation Data Lake; there are several other components that need to be built to realize the vision. In this section, we will see the core capabilities that need to be built in order to enable an Enterprise Data Lake. The following are the key components that need to be built for an effective Data Lake:

Let us look into each component in detail.

Ingestion and organization

Data Lake based on HDFS has a scalable and distributed filesystem that requires a scalable ingestion framework and software that can take in structured, unstructured, and streaming data.

A managed Data Lake requires data to be well-organized and this requires several kinds of metadata. The following are key metadata that require management:

- **File inventory**: What, when, and who about files ingested to Hadoop?

- **Structural metadata**: What is the structure of a file such as XML, HL7, CSV, and TSV?

 Hadoop does work well with Avro sequence file where the metadata and data are stored together.

- **User-defined information**: Additional information that the user is provided with such as comments and tags for a file.

Transformation (rules driven)

A key design consideration for next generation Data Lakes is easy for building new transformations as demanded by business. This requires a workflow to orchestrate the sequence of rules-based transformations; where business users can author rules.

Access, analyze, and report

To democratize access to data from a Data Lake, the following patterns of access need to be enabled:

- **Direct data access**: Access to data via programs and ad hoc queries for power users via tools

- **BI tools**: Access via BI tools for dashboards and reports

Tools and technology for Hadoop ecosystem

Next generation architecture includes Hadoop-based projects that complement the traditional RDBMS systems. The following table highlights key projects that are organized by Data Lake capabilities:

Capability	Tool	Description
Ingest	Flume	This is a distributed and reliable software to collect large amounts of data from different sources such as logfiles in a streaming fashion in Hadoop.
Ingest	Sqoop	This tool is designed to transfer data between Hadoop and RDBMS such as Oracle, Teradata, and SQL Server.
Organize	HCatalog	This tool stores metadata for Hadoop, including file structures and formats. It provides an abstraction and interoperability across various tools such as Pig, MapReduce, Hive, Impala, and others.
Tranform	Oozie	This is a workflow scheduler system to manage Apache Hadoop jobs, which can be MapReduce, Hive, Pig, and others. It provides developers greater control over complex jobs and also makes it easier to repeat those at predetermined intervals.
Transform	YARN	With Hadoop 2.*x*, YARN takes over all the resource management capabilities on top of Hadoop so that it can now serve broad types of workloads such as batch, interactive, streaming, in-memory, and others.
Transform and Access	Pig	A scripting language such as Python that abstracts MapReduce and is useful for data scientists.
Transform	Spark	This is a fast and general compute engine for Hadoop with a **directed acyclic graph (DAG)** execution engine that supports complex data flows and in-memory computing. There are number of tools and projects that now leverage Spark as their execution engine, for example, Talend, which is an ETL tool.
Transform	Tez	Tez is a framework that allows complex DAG of tasks for processing data using native YARN APIs. It is designed to empower end users by providing expressive dataflow definitions and has significant performance gains over MapReduce.

Capability	Tool	Description
Access	Hive	Data warehouse infrastructure that provides SQL-like access on HDFS. This is suited for ad hoc queries on Hadoop that abstract MapReduce.
Access	Excel	With HDInsight, you can connect Excel to HDFS via Hive queries using ODBC to analyze and visualize your data.
Access	Mahout	This framework allows machine learning and data mining on top of Hadoop.
Operations	Ambari	A Web-based provisioning, managing, and monitoring tool for Hadoop cluster. It also provides a dashboard with cluster health and the ability to see current running jobs in a user-friendly manner.

Use case powered by Microsoft HDInsight

Let's take a look at a practical use case powered by Microsoft HDInsight that demonstrates the value of next generation Data Lake architecture.

Problem statement

The Virginia Bioinformatics Institute collaborates with institutes across the globe to locate undetected genes in a massive genome database that leads to exciting medical breakthroughs such as cancer therapies. This database size is growing exponentially across the 2,000 DNA sequencers and is generating 15 petabytes of genome data every year. Several universities lack storage and compute resources to handle this kind of workload in a timely and cost-effective manner.

Solution

The institute built a solution on top of Windows Azure HDInsight service to perform DNA sequencing analysis in the cloud. This enabled the team to analyze petabytes of data in a cost-effective and scalable manner. Let's take a look at how the Data Lake reference architecture applies to this use case. The following figure shows you the solution architecture:

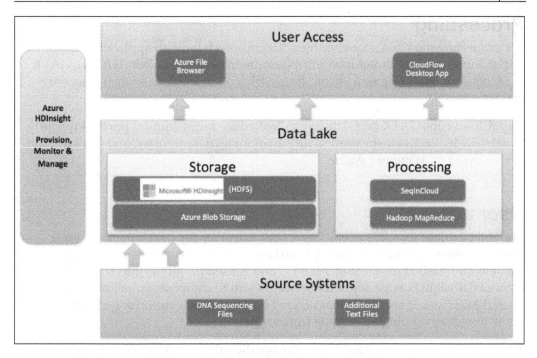

Let's review the stack in detail.

Source systems

Source data for the initiative are various DNA sequence files and additional text files that are generally from researchers' desktop machines.

Storage

All big data was stored in the Azure cloud ecosystem thereby reducing the need for an in-house data center. Azure Blob storage was used to persist data, independent of HDInsight cluster; this resulted in additional cost savings by only paying for the HDInsight compute services on-demand without the loss of any data.

Processing

For processing the DNA sequence files, Virginia Tech built an application called SeqInCloud based on Broad Institute's **Genome Analysis Toolkit (GATK)**. GATK is a toolkit for analyzing sequencing data with a main focus on variant discovery and genotyping.

SeqInCloud runs GATK on HDInsight MapReduce for maximum portability and scalability. It also has features for data partitioning, data transfer, and storage optimization on Windows Azure.

User access

The end customers for this project were data scientists for which the team built another custom application called **CloudFlow**. This is a workflow management framework installed on a researcher's PC and is used for all the interactions with Azure HDInsight Service. CloudFlow allows you to compose a pipeline with several MapReduce segments that utilize both client and cloud resources and allow user-defined plugins for data transformation.

The users can also access Azure Blob storage directly from a browser that allows collaboration across different stakeholders.

Benefits

The solution based on HDInsight for DNA sequencing has several benefits out of which the key ones are listed as follows:

- **Scalable solution**: As the cluster is on Azure cloud, it can be scaled to higher number of nodes if the demand and data volumes increase.

- **Shorter time for analysis**: With HDInsight, the team was able to analyze DNA sequences in an effective and timely manner.

- **Significant cost savings**: When compared to millions of dollars required to build a data center to handle this work load, the Azure HDInsight service has proven to be a cost-effective alternative. Since data is stored in Azure Blob storage, the cluster can be torn down but data is still preserved for future reference thereby further reducing the compute expenses.

- **Improved collaboration**: Since data is stored in the cloud, sharing public datasets became really easy with other researchers spread across the country. Additionally, data can be accessed by various types of end devices, which include mobile phones and tablets. This approach leads to new opportunities such as genome analysis at a hospital, which could lead to faster, prescribed treatments.

- **Easy visualization impact**: With HDInsight, business users benefited from quick visualization using Power BI dashboards with Office 365 / Excel 2013 and were able to analyze data in a better and faster way.

The **National Human Genome Research Institute (NHGRI)** has been tracking costs associated with DNA sequencing since 2001 and the following figure shows you the trend due to such innovations in universities such as Virginia Tech:

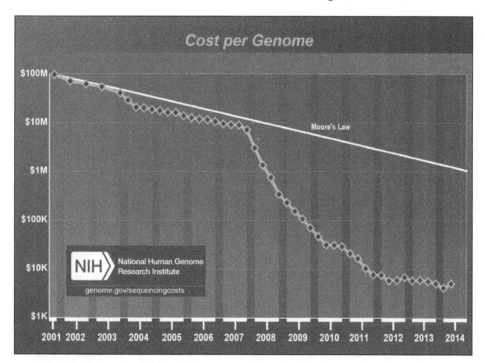

Source: http://www.genome.gov/sequencingcosts/

 For more information, you can refer to http://www.microsoft. com/casestudies/Windows-Azure/Virginia-Polytechnic-Institute-and-State-University/University-Transforms-Life-Sciences-Research-with-Big-Data-Solution-in-the-Cloud/710000003381.

Summary

Most organizations have built expensive EDWs as the centralized data repositories serving critical business decisions. The relational EDW-based architecture is struggling to handle the data growth and ability to provide near real-time metrics. Hadoop-based Data Lake has emerged as a cost-effective alternative to EDW providing access to real-time information to business users in a more agile fashion.

Microsoft HDInsight Azure-based service is well-positioned to enable a modern Data Lake on the cloud thereby further reducing operational and data center costs.

In the next chapter, we will build, configure, and monitor a new HDInsight cluster, which is the first step in building a Data Lake.

3
HDInsight Service on Azure

Microsoft Azure is a flexible cloud platform that enables enterprises of any size to quickly rent resources on demand to build, deploy, and manage a wide range of IT applications. HDInsight is a 100 percent Apache Hadoop-based cloud service that leverages the Azure platform.

In this chapter, we will discuss how to build your Data Lake using the HDInsight service on the Azure cloud, which can scale to petabytes on demand. We will cover the following topics:

- Registering for an Azure account
- Provisioning an HDInsight cluster
- HDInsight Management dashboard
- Exploring a cluster using the remote desktop
- Deleting the HDInsight cluster
- HDInsight Emulator for development

Registering for an Azure account

The first step to access the HDInsight cloud service is to open an account with Microsoft Azure.

From the Microsoft Azure management portal, you can get information about the features, pricing, documentation, and support on various services provided by Azure. HDInsight is one of these services grouped under data management services.

The following steps show you how to estimate the monthly pricing for an HDInsight cluster:

1. Click on **Pricing**.

2. Next, click on the **data management** icon.

3. Next, you can select the desired configuration **Two Head Nodes on an Extra Large (A4) instance included** or **Two Head Nodes on a Large (A3) instance included**. The head nodes will host the master Hadoop services that include HDFS NameNode, YARN ResourceManager, and other central services.

4. Next, you can slide the bar, as shown in the following screenshot, to change the number of compute nodes. The compute nodes are the worker nodes and will host the data nodes and YARN NodeManager services.

5. In the following screenshot, I have selected extra large head nodes and 2 compute nodes. The price you see is the average monthly cost, which is $1,428.48 based on $1.92/hour and assuming 31 days and each day has 24 hours.

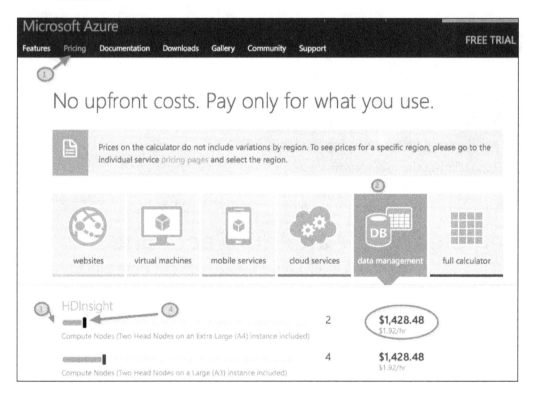

Azure storage

Before you provision a new HDInsight cluster, it is required that you create a storage account in Azure. To create a new storage account, first login to the Microsoft Azure management portal and then follow the given steps, as shown in the following screenshot:

1. Click on **STORAGE** on the left-hand side menu.

2. Click on **CREATE STORAGE ACCOUNT**.

3. Select your preferences, which are as follows:

    ° **URL** must be a unique name

    ° Location should be ideally geographically closer to your data center to reduce network latency

    ° Replication mode, where you can select from one of the following four options:

    ° **Locally Redundant Storage (LRS)** where data is replicated in three different nodes within the same region.

    ° **Geo-Redundant Storage (GRS)**, which is similar to LRS, replicates data three times within the local region; however, the transactions also get queued to a remote secondary region that is hundreds of miles away from the primary site.

    ° **Read Access Geo-Redundant Storage (RA-GRS)**, which is an improved version of GRS, allows read-only access to the storage data in the secondary region.

    ° **Zone Redundant Storage (ZRS)**, which fits between LRS and GRS in terms of durability and price. ZRS stores three replicas of data across two or three facilities but typically in the same region.

    ° For the test cluster, I have selected the **Locally Redundant** option.

4. Click on **CREATE STORAGE ACCOUNT** to finally create it:

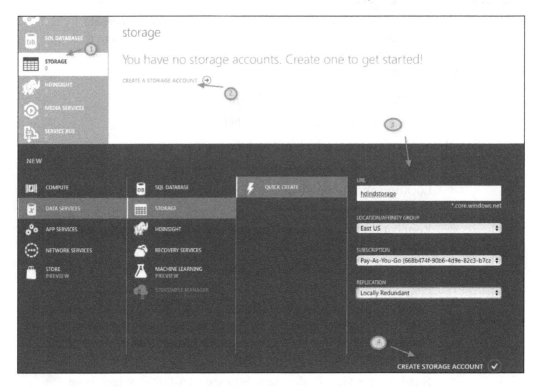

Provisioning an HDInsight cluster

After the storage is successfully created online, we can create an HDInsight cluster. From the Azure Management Portal, select **HDInsight** and click on **CREATE HDINSIGHT CLUSTER**. Perform the following detailed steps, which are shown in the following screenshot:

1. Click on the Hadoop Menu option, which is used for quick creation. If you need customized settings, then you can use **CUSTOM CREATE**.

 HDInsight does have additional options for HBase and Storm, which we will review in *Chapter 8, HDInsight 3.1 New Features*.

2. Select a unique cluster name that should be a word between 3 and 63 characters and can support letters, numbers, and hyphens only. I have selected `hdind` and the complete URL is `hdind.azurehdinsight.net`.

3. Select the desired number of data nodes in the cluster. Currently, Azure supports 1, 2, 4, 8, 16, and 32 nodes.

4. Next, select a password for the cluster. The password must be at least 10 characters, including one uppercase letter, one lowercase letter, one number, and one special character. The default administration user for accessing the cluster is Admin.

5. Next, select the storage. I have selected the **hdindstorage** that was created in the previous section.

6. Next, click on **CREATE HDINSIGHT CLUSTER** at the bottom right-hand corner.

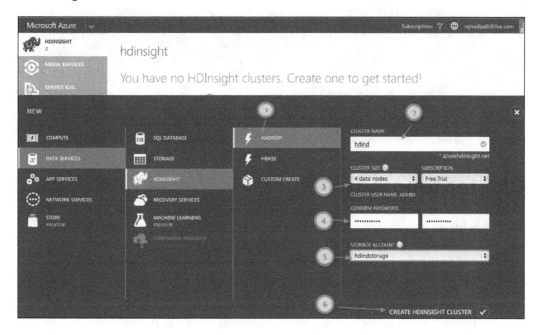

Next, you need to wait for Azure to provision the cluster; this step will take 10 minutes, after which you will see a message that the cluster is up and running, as shown in the following screenshot:

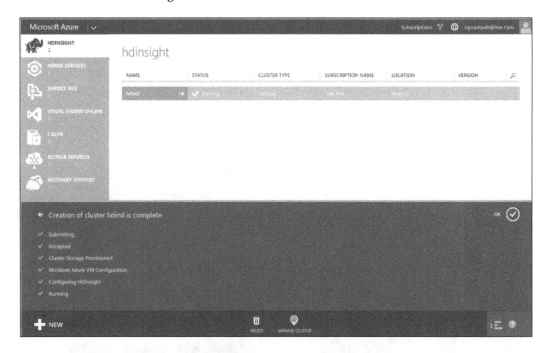

Cluster topology

With the default four-node configuration, HDInsight will assign four virtual machines for worker nodes and two machines for head nodes (second one for High Availability). The head node handles the critical services, which are Hadoop NameNode and Yarn ResourceManager. Worker nodes handle the data node and YARN application containers.

HDInsight differs from the traditional Hadoop model, where storage and compute are intertwined. In HDInsight, you can add more storage via Azure Blob storage with the same compute capacity or increase the compute worker nodes with the same Azure storage.

The high-speed flat network in the Azure data center provides fast access between the nodes and the Azure Blob storage so the data movement is very efficient. The Azure team has conducted tests that show that the performance of the read operation to Blob storage is identical to HDFS with local storage and the writes to Azure Blob is generally better than HDFS with local storage (for more information, visit http://msdn.microsoft.com/en-us/library/dn749864.aspx).

HDInsight comes, by default, with two head nodes. The second head node is added to increase the availability of the service for High Availability. The switch to HA doesn't change the cluster pricing.

The following figure shows you the topology of the four-node cluster:

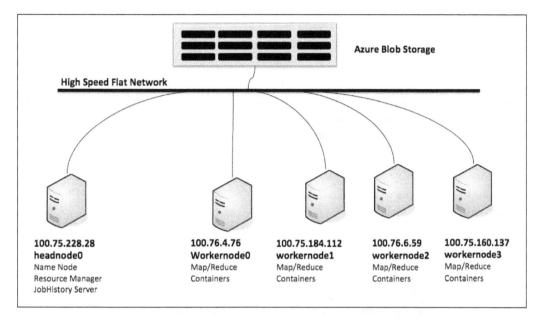

Provisioning using Azure PowerShell

Azure PowerShell is a scripting environment that can be used to provision a new HDInsight cluster. In this section, we will review how to create a new storage container and provision a new HDInsight cluster.

You can download and install this component on any Windows machine using the link http://go.microsoft.com/fwlink/p/?LinkID=320376.

After the installation is complete, launch the Azure PowerShell application and then perform the following steps to create the storage container and the cluster.

Creating a storage container

HDInsight uses an Azure Blob storage container as the default filesystem. Use the following commands to create a new container:

```
# Get PublishSettingsFile, this opens a browser window
Get-AzurePublishSettingsFile


# Import PublishSettingsFile that was saved from last step
Import-AzurePublishSettingsFile "C:\Users\Administrator\Downloads\Pay-As-You-Go-Free Trial-11-21-2014-credentials.publishsettings"


# Set Subscription Name and Current Storage
Set-AzureSubscription -SubscriptionName "Pay-As-You-Go"
-CurrentStorageAccount "hdindstorage"


# Set the storage variables
$storageAccountName = "hdindstorage"

$containerName = "hdind-3"

$destContext = New-AzureStorageContext -StorageAccountName
$storageAccountName -StorageAccountKey $storageAccountKey


# Create a Blob storage container
New-AzureStorageContainer -Name $containerName -Context $destContext
```

The preceding set of commands will create the new storage container hdind-3, as shown in the following screenshot:

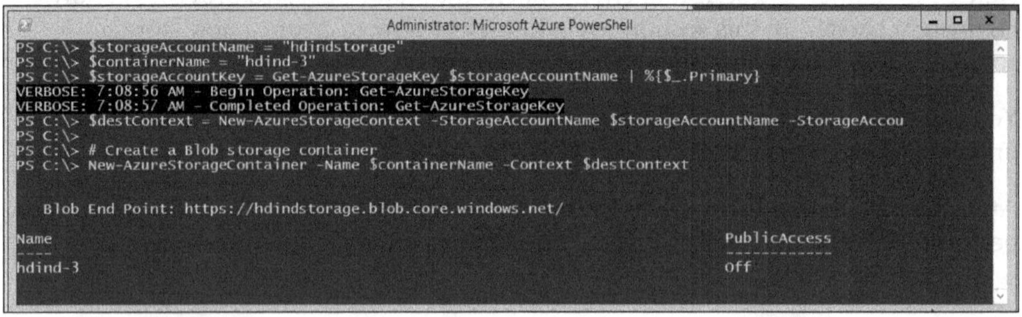

Provisioning a new HDInsight cluster

The next step is to provision the cluster. The following commands will help you create a new HDInsight cluster:

```
#Get the storage account key
$storageAccountKey = Get-AzureStorageKey $storageAccountName | %{$_.
Primary}


# Set New cluster properties
$clusterName = "hdind2"
$location = "West US"
$clusterNodes = 1


# Create new cluster
New-AzureHDInsightCluster -Name $clusterName -Location $location
-DefaultStorageAccountName "$storageAccountName.blob.core.windows.net"
-DefaultStorageAccountKey $storageAccountKey -DefaultStorageContainerName
$containerName   -ClusterSizeInNodes $clusterNodes
```

The preceding commands will provision the hdind2 cluster, as shown in the following screenshot:

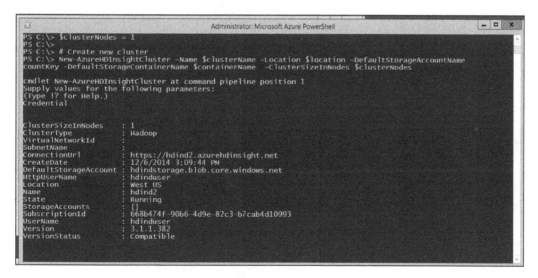

HDInsight management dashboard

Once the cluster is created, we can view the dashboard by clicking on the cluster name **hdind** in our case. This has three major areas: dashboard, monitor, and configuration.

Dashboard

The **DASHBOARD** page displays a summary of the cluster, current usage, and linked storage information, as shown in the following screenshot. The notable mentions on the **DASHBOARD** page are as follows:

- The graph shows you two trend lines: one in brown for YARN applications and another in blue for containers used by the application. For each line, you will see the total and actual number in use. The time frame of this graph can be changed from the default 1 hour to 4 hours or day relative or absolute.

- The **quick glance** section shows you the cluster location, cluster URL, version, and data node count.

- The linked resources section identifies the underlying Azure storage.

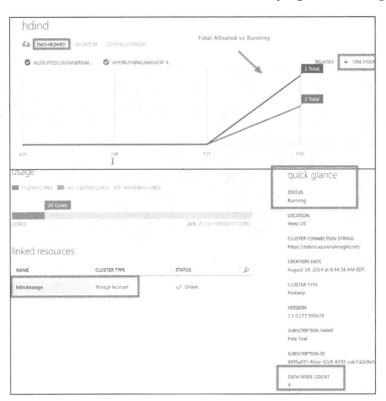

Monitor

The **MONITOR** tab is the second tab of the HDInsight management dashboard that currently shows the running applications along with stats of max, min, and average times. The following screenshot shows you the monitoring page:

Configuration

The third tab in the HDInsight management dashboard is **CONFIGURATION** and is shown in the following screenshot. HDInsight clusters with the following HTTP web services can be turned on/off using the configuration page: ODBC, JDBC, Ambari, Oozie, and Templeton. You can use this page to turn the **HADOOP SERVICES** option off by clicking on the **OFF** button and then clicking on **Save**.

Another useful button on this page is **ENABLE REMOTE**, which can be used to connect to the cluster remotely using a remote desktop connection to the head node:

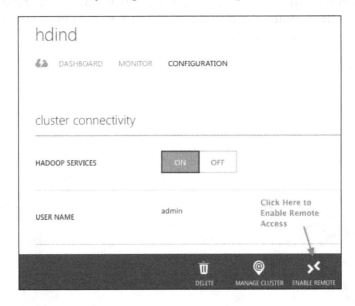

After you click on the **ENABLE REMOTE** button, you will be prompted to enter a username that does not already exist on the head node server and assign a password and then to set an expiration date, which must be seven days or less from today. You need to save your settings to preserve the configuration. The following screenshot shows you the **Configure Remote Desktop** pop-up menu:

Exploring clusters using the remote desktop

Once the cluster is up and running, the best way to explore it is via the remote desktop. This section discusses how to check the cluster status using Hadoop commands in detail. From the HDInsight **CONFIGURATION** page, you can download the RDP file by clicking on **CONNECT**, as shown in the following screenshot. This RDP file allows one to connect to the active head node remotely.

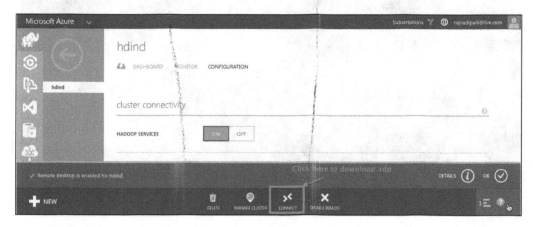

The next step is to launch the remote desktop to the head node by opening the .rdp file with a remote desktop connection application. On launching the application, it will prompt you for a username and password, which you entered in the remote desktop connection configuration.

Once you get connected, you will see the familiar Windows desktop, as shown in the following screenshot:

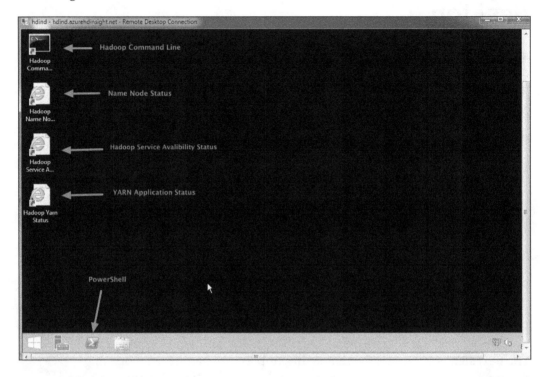

Running a sample MapReduce

Using the Hadoop Command Line interface, we can verify the cluster by running a sample program provided by HDInsight. Let's take a look at the steps to run the famous Hadoop Wordcount MapReduce program that counts the word occurrences in a text file:

1. First, launch the Hadoop Command Line using the shortcut on the desktop.

2. Next, to run Wordcount, we will use the sample text file as the input /example/data/gutenberg/davinci.txt. Once the MapReduce job completes, the output file is created in Hadoop as per the last argument, which is shown in the following example as /usr/rajn/WordCountOutput/ part-r-00000.

The following commands show you the execution of the `Wordcount` MapReduce job:

```
C:\apps\dist\hadoop-2.4.0.2.1.3.3-0025>hadoop jar hadoop-mapreduce-
examples.jar wordcount /example/data/gutenberg/davinci.txt/usr/rajn/
WordCountOutput


14/08/22 01:35:20 INFO client.RMProxy: Connecting to ResourceManager at
headnode
host/100.74.170.53:9010
14/08/22 01:35:22 INFO input.FileInputFormat: Total input paths to
process : 1
14/08/22 01:35:22 INFO mapreduce.JobSubmitter: number of splits:1
14/08/22 01:35:22 INFO mapreduce.JobSubmitter: Submitting tokens for job:
job_1408668140066_0001
14/08/22 01:35:23 INFO impl.YarnClientImpl: Submitted application
application_1408668140066_0001
14/08/22 01:35:23 INFO mapreduce.Job: The url to track the job: http://
headnodehost:9014/proxy/application_1408668140066_0001/
14/08/22 01:35:23 INFO mapreduce.Job: Running job: job_1408668140066_0001
14/08/22 01:35:35 INFO mapreduce.Job: Job job_1408668140066_0001 running
in ubermode : false
14/08/22 01:35:35 INFO mapreduce.Job:  map 0% reduce 0%
14/08/22 01:35:47 INFO mapreduce.Job:  map 100% reduce 0%
14/08/22 01:36:01 INFO mapreduce.Job:  map 100% reduce 100%
14/08/22 01:36:03 INFO mapreduce.Job: Job job_1408668140066_0001
completed successfully
```

The following commands show you the output of the `Wordcount` MapReduce job:

```
                C:\apps\dist\hadoop-2.4.0.2.1.3.3-0025>hadoop fs -ls /usr/
rajn/WordCountOutput

Found 2 items

-rw-r--r--    1 rajn supergroup           0 2014-08-22 01:35 /usr/rajn/
WordC

ountOutput/_SUCCESS

-rw-r--r--    1 rajn supergroup      337623 2014-08-22 01:35 /usr/rajn/
WordC

ountOutput/part-r-00000


C:\apps\dist\hadoop-2.4.0.2.1.3.3-0025>hadoop fs -cat /usr/rajn/
WordCountOutput/

part-r-00000 | more

"(Lo)cra"       1

"1490    1

"1498,"  1

"35"     1
```

```
"40,"    1
"AS-IS".       1
"A_      1
"Absoluti      1
"Alack! 1
"Alack!"       1
"Alla    1
"Allegorical   1
"Alpine-glow"  1
"And     2
"Antoni 1
"At      1
"B_      1
```

The following screenshot shows you the execution of the MapReduce job from the Hadoop Command Line window:

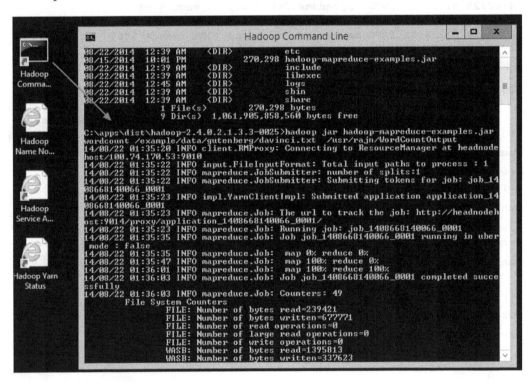

Deleting the cluster

An HDInsight cluster is charged per hour of usage; hence, it is recommended that you delete your cluster if you are not using those resources. One great feature of Azure is that your data is still preserved on Azure Blob storage even after the cluster is deleted, and this storage can be used later to restore back your cluster. If you really want to delete all the data of your cluster, you need to delete the related Azure storage.

The following screenshot shows you the location of the **DELETE** icon for the cluster:

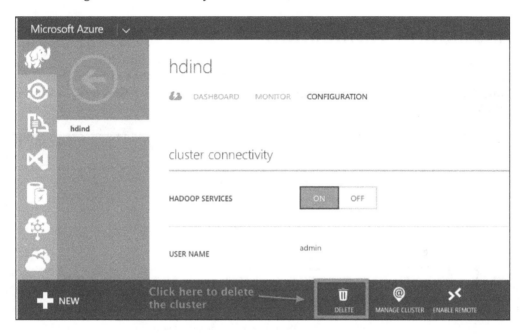

HDInsight Emulator for the development

HDInsight Emulator is the development edition of Azure HDInsight that runs locally on the Windows desktop and servers. It is essentially a single node Hadoop cluster where storage and compute reside on the same machine unlike the Azure cloud HDInsight service, where a cluster consists of multiple nodes and storage is on Azure Blob storage.

HDInsight Emulator is supported by the following 64-bit operating systems: Windows 7 Service Pack 1, Windows Server 2008 R2 Service Pack1, Windows 8, or Windows Server 2012.

Installing HDInsight Emulator

To install HDInsight Emulator, open a browser and enter the URL `http://www.microsoft.com/web/gallery/install.aspx?appid=HDINSIGHT`.

The installation is a wizard driven by Microsoft Web Platform Installer (WebPI) and will install and configure the required dependencies. The complete installation process will take several minutes depending on your Internet connection and your system resources. After the completion, you might be asked to restart your computer.

Installation verification

Once HDInsight Emulator is installed, the services are registered with Windows System like other services and can be stopped and started through **Control Panel | System and Security | Administrative Tools | Services**, as shown in the following screenshot:

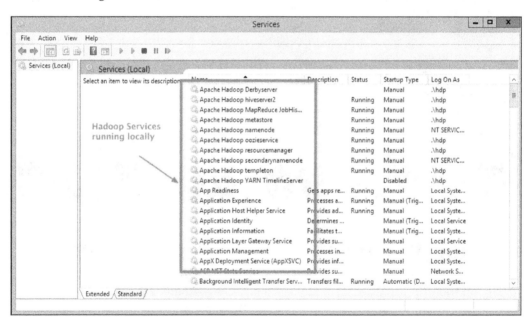

Using HDInsight Emulator

To use an HDInsight single node cluster, you can use the familiar Hadoop Command Line, Hadoop Name Node Status, and Hadoop YARN Status; similar to the one seen in the Azure cloud HDInsight service. The following screenshot shows you the shortcuts on the HDInsight single node install:

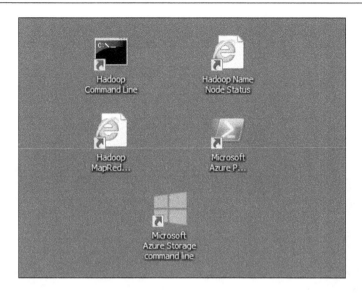

Summary

In this chapter, we looked at how to open a new Microsoft Azure account, create a
new HDInsight service, and run sample jobs on the HDInsight cluster in the cloud.
Next, we looked at how an HDInsight Hadoop cluster allows scaling of storage and
compute independently, making the solution flexible and cost effective. Lastly, we
looked at a single node HDInsight Emulator, which is great for development and can
be installed on the local desktop.

Now that the cluster is up and running, we will look at how to administer and
monitor it in the next chapter.

4
Administering Your HDInsight Cluster

In the previous chapter, we looked at how to manage an HDInsight cluster using the Azure management portal. In this chapter, we will review how to access and manage the cluster using a remote desktop connection. We will cover the following topics:

- Monitoring cluster health
- Name Node status
- Yarn application status
- Azure storage management
- Azure PowerShell

Monitoring cluster health

To ensure that development has a stable Hadoop environment, the operations team should have visibility of the cluster status, including the health of various services in a programmatic manner. This section discusses how to monitor an HDInsight cluster using remote connection to the head node in detail. From the HDInsight **CONFIGURATION** page, you can download the RDP file to connect to the head node remotely.

Once connected, you will see the familiar Windows desktop, as shown in the following screenshot:

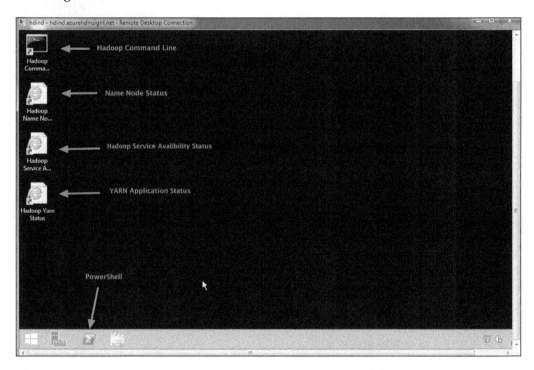

There are four key shortcuts on the remote desktop that help you monitor and manage the cluster. The following table lists the different shortcuts and their purpose:

Link name	URL	Purpose
Hadoop Command Line	None	This is a Windows command line shortcut to run any Hadoop command such as listing of files or calling MapReduce program
Hadoop Name Node Status	`http:// headnodehost:30070`	This lists the Hadoop Name Node status and summary statistics
Hadoop Service Availability Status	`http:// headnodehost/ ServiceAvailability`	This lists all the Hadoop services
Hadoop Yarn Status	`http:// headnodehost:9014/ cluster`	This lists the Hadoop Yarn application status, including MapReduce jobs

The first shortcut from the remote desktop is the Hadoop Command Line. This shortcut will launch the familiar Windows Command Prompt ready for any Hadoop command to interact with the distributed filesystem (HDFS). The following is the list of all the HDFS commands:

```
appendToFile, cat, chgrp, chmod, chown, copyFromLocal,
copyToLocal, count, cp, du. dus, expunge, get, getfacl, getfattr,
getmerge, ls, lsr, mkdir, moveFromLocal, moveToLocal, mv, put, rm, rmr,
setfacl, setfattr, setrep, stat, tail, test, text, touchz
```

Let's take a look at the following example:

```
hadoop fs -mkdir /user/guest/newdirectory
```

In the next few sections, we will review the other shortcuts in detail.

Name Node status

The second shortcut from the remote desktop is Hadoop Name Node Status, which gives you the details of the NameNode. This URL can be accessed from any node of the cluster using the address `http://headnodehost:30070`.

The Name Node status web page has the following key menu items:

- Name Node overview
- Datanode status
- Utilities and logs

The other menu items include snapshots and startup progress. Let's take a look at the key menu items in detail.

The Name Node Overview page

The Name Node **Overview** page gives us the following important information:

- The cluster identifier, Hadoop version, and the date when it was started
- The total storage capacity, percentage used, and available storage
- The total number of nodes alive and decommissioned
- The location of Name Node metadata, which includes the journal entries for files, blocks, and their replicas

The following screenshot shows you the first section of the **Overview** tab where the key information is the cluster ID and the start date and time:

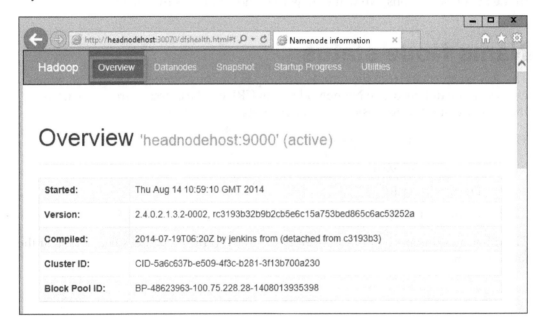

The next section of the **Overview** page reports the following key information: DFS (distributed file system) total space, DFS percent used, and number of active nodes:

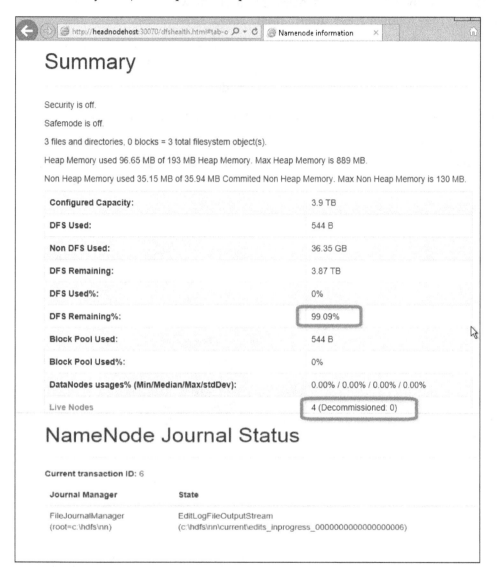

Datanode Status

Datanodes is the next tab on the Name Node status web page. From this page, we can get the following key information:

- Listing of each active worker node along with its IP address, total capacity, and available storage
- Listing of decommissioned worker nodes

In the following screenshot, you can see a Name Node status web page:

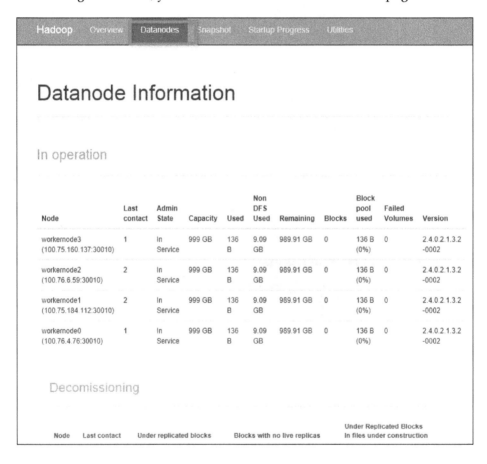

Utilities and logs

Another key menu option on the Name Node status web page is called **Utilities**, as shown in the following screenshot. From this menu, you can browse the filesystem and see the logs.

The following screenshot shows you the list of logs accessible from the **Logs** submenu:

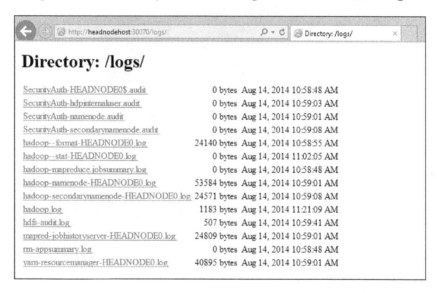

Hadoop Service Availability

The third shortcut from the remote desktop is Hadoop Service Availability, which gives you a list of all the key services and where each one is running. The following screenshot shows you the content of the web page:

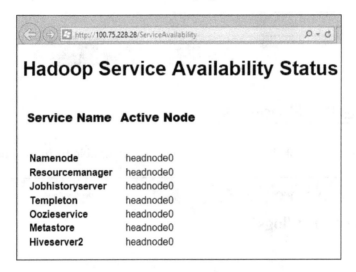

YARN Application Status

The fourth shortcut from the remote desktop is the YARN application status, which provides you with details on all applications that are submitted, running, and completed. The following screenshot shows you the YARN status web page, which is available at `http://headnodehost:9014/cluster`:

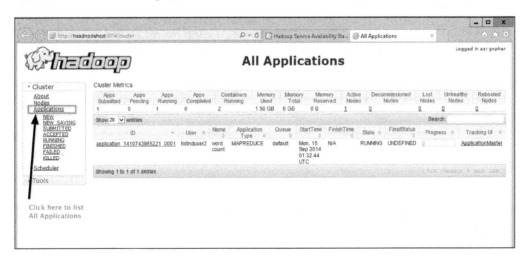

To get the details of any particular application such as a MapReduce job, you can click on the **History** link, as shown in the following screenshot:

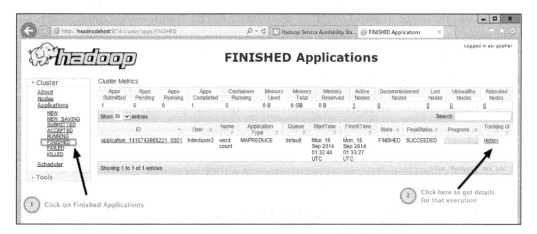

The following screenshot shows you the details of a MapReduce job, which includes status, start time, end time, number of map containers, and number of reduce containers:

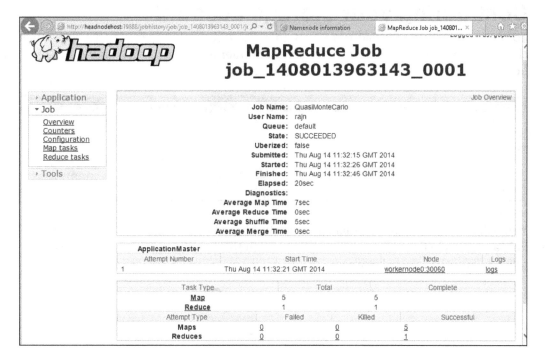

Azure storage management

Windows Azure storage is a cloud storage solution that abstracts physical storage and allows end users to build scalable applications. The Windows HDInsight service leverages Azure Blob storage but still provides all the HDFS command line and other programming interfaces.

Azure storage has the following characteristics:

- Cost effective, as you only have to pay for what you use
- Scalable and flexible, as you can scale up or down your application based on your business needs
- Replicated based on your requirements either locally or geo-replicated at another distant data center
- Highly available, as multiple replicas provide fault tolerance
- Accessible via REST API

Let's take a look at how to manage and monitor your Azure storage.

Configuring your storage account

To configure your storage account, first go to the Azure management portal and then click on the **STORAGE** icon from the left-hand menu and next, click on the storage **hdindstorage**, as shown in the following screenshot:

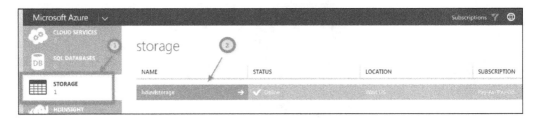

You will then see the storage management dashboard page. Click on the **CONFIGURE** link, as shown in the following screenshot. From this page, you can configure the following for the selected storage:

- **Replication**: You can choose from LRS, where replication is within the same region; GRS, which is similar to LRS, in addition, the transactions also get queued to a remote secondary region; or RA-GRS, which is an improved version of GRS, and it allows read access to a secondary region.

- **Monitoring**: Using the configuration page, you can change the level of monitoring. As HDInsight only uses Blobs, I have updated the level to minimal, as shown in the following screenshot.

- **Logging**: Additionally, you can change the logging levels for Blobs, using the configuration page, as shown in the following screenshot:

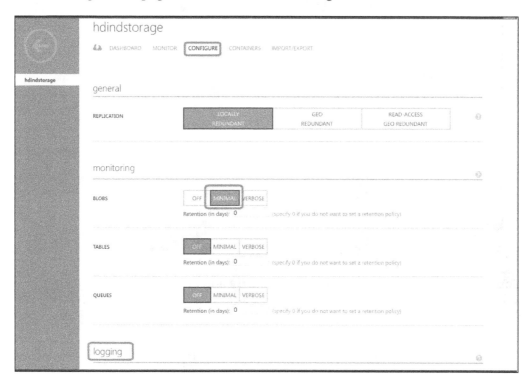

Monitoring your storage account

To monitor the storage account, click on the **MONITOR** tab, which is to the left of the **CONFIGURE** tab, as shown in the following screenshot:

You can add additional metrics such as **Capacity** and also add alert rules on top of a metric such as its capacity is greater than a threshold, as shown in the following screenshot:

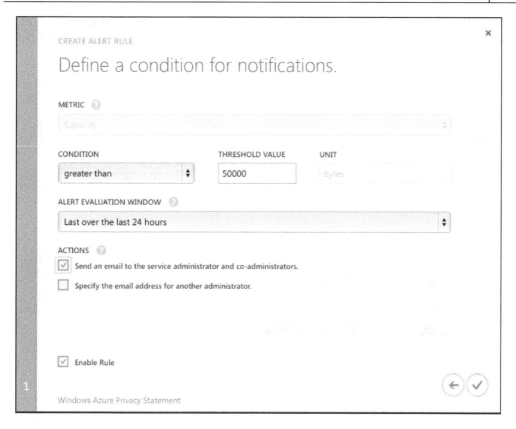

CREATE ALERT RULE

Define a condition for notifications.

METRIC

Capacity

CONDITION | THRESHOLD VALUE | UNIT

greater than | 50000 | Bytes

ALERT EVALUATION WINDOW

Last over the last 24 hours

ACTIONS

☑ Send an email to the service administrator and co-administrators.

☐ Specify the email address for another administrator.

☑ Enable Rule

Windows Azure Privacy Statement

Managing access keys

Azure storage can be accessed by several open source and commercial software such as Azure Storage Explorer (`https://azurestorageexplorer.codeplex.com/`).

To access it, you need the account information and keys that can be set from the **Manage Access Keys** icon found in the footer of the Monitor/Configure page.

This will open the pop-up screen that contains the storage name, and primary and secondary keys, as shown in the following screenshot. Using this pop-up menu, you can regenerate the keys if required.

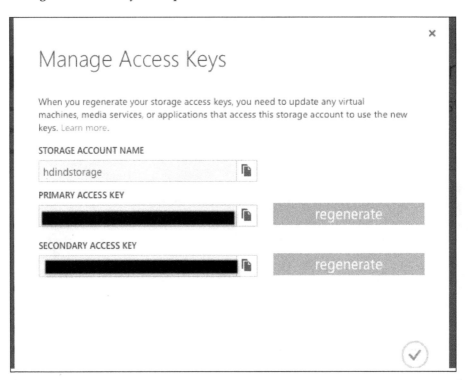

Deleting your storage account

To remove a storage account, click on the **DELETE** icon, which is in the footer of the **CONFIGURATION** page. This will delete the entire storage account, including all of the Blobs, tables, and queues in the account.

 There is no way to restore the storage once it is deleted, so backup the data before you delete it.

Azure PowerShell

Azure PowerShell is a scripting environment that can be used to automate the deployment and management of your workloads in Azure from a remote machine such as your laptop. You can download and install this component on any Windows machine, using the link `http://go.microsoft.com/fwlink/p/?LinkID=320376`.

 The HDInsight Emulator installation includes the Azure PowerShell component.

Access Azure Blob storage using Azure PowerShell

In this section, we will use Azure PowerShell from the local Windows laptop to the Azure cloud subscription. Perform the following the steps to access Azure Blob storage using Azure PowerShell:

1. Using the Windows Emulator machine, launch the Microsoft Azure PowerShell using the desktop shortcut, as shown in the following screenshot:

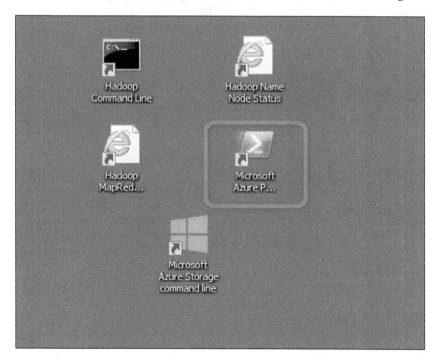

2. In the new Azure PowerShell prompt, type in the following command:

```
Get-AzurePublishSettingsFile
```

This will launch your browser and prompt you to log in to your Azure account and then will automatically download a management certificate for all your subscriptions. Make a note of the location and filename of the file.

3. Next, type in the following command in the Azure PowerShell prompt to import the publish settings file:

```
Import-AzurePublishSettingsFile "C:\Users\Username\Downloads\Pay-
As-You-Go-credentials.publishsettings"
```

4. If you have multiple Azure subscriptions, you will need to use the `Set-AzureSubscription` command to the context of PowerShell:

```
Set-AzureSubscription -SubscriptionName "Pay-As-You-Go"
-CurrentStorageAccount "hdindstorage"
```

5. Next, get the storage account key using the `Get-AzureStorageKey` command and set the storage context:

```
$storageAccountKey = Get-AzureStorageKey $storageAccountName |
%{$_.Primary}
```

```
$storageContext = New-AzureStorageContext -StorageAccountName
$storageAccountName -StorageAccountKey $storageAccountKey
```

6. Next, set the container name and `blobprefix`:

```
$containerName = "hdind-1"
```

```
$blobPrefix = "example/data/"
```

7. Next, to get a file listing for a directory, use the `Get-AzureStorageBlob` command:

```
Get-AzureStorageBlob -Container $containerName -Context
$storageContext -prefix $blobPrefix
```

The following screenshot shows you the commands in action:

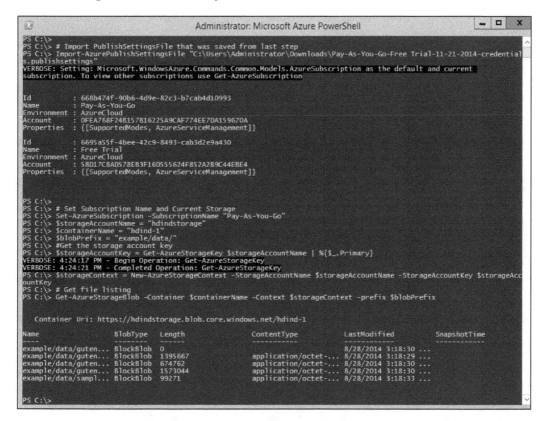

 HDInsight provides you with the ability to access data stored in the Blob storage, using the following syntax:

```
wasb[s]://<containername>@<accountname>.blob.core.
windows.net/<path>
```

Summary

For a healthy HDInsight cluster, the operations team needs to routinely review the cluster Name Node status, YARN application status, and Azure storage. The best way to monitor it is by remotely connecting to the head node. Azure PowerShell provides you additional capability to script and automate monitoring from any Windows machine. In the next chapter, we will look at how to ingest data to the newly created cluster.

5
Ingest and Organize Data Lake

In this chapter, we will look at how to ingest and organize data to the newly created Data Lake to make it effective and useful. The topics covered in this chapter are as follows:

- End-to-end Data Lake solution
- Ingest data using HDFS commands
- Ingest data to Azure Blob using Azure PowerShell
- Ingest data using CloudXplorer
- Using Sqoop to move data from RDBMS to cluster
- Organizing your data in HDFS
- Managing metadata using HCatalog

End-to-end Data Lake solution

In the next few chapters, we will build an end-to-end Data Lake solution using HDInsight. As discussed in *Chapter 2*, *Enterprise Data Lake using HDInsight*, the three key components required for a Data Lake are:

- Ingest and organize
- Transform
- Access, analyze, and report

To understand these concepts, we will use real flight on-time performance data from the RITA website with the URL http://www.transtats.bts.gov/DL_SelectFields.asp?Table_ID=236.

In this chapter, we will focus on ingest and organize components:

Ingesting to Data Lake using HDFS command

The simplest way to upload files is to use Hadoop command line. The following are the steps to load data into Data Lake.

Connecting to a Hadoop client

You can connect to the Hadoop cluster via a remote desktop connection to the active head node. After establishing the remote connection, launch the Hadoop command-line application that can be found as a shortcut on the desktop.

Getting your files on the local storage

Get your files on the edge node, either via web download, SCP or SFTP. The following figure shows you the steps to download the on-time performance data from the website. The steps are selecting the year, month, and other similar fields and then clicking on **Download**. The fields that we need for the project are listed as follows:

YEAR, QUARTER, MONTH, DAY_OF_MONTH, DAY_OF_WEEK, FL_DATE, UNIQUE_CARRIER, AIRLINE_ID, FL_NUM, ORIGIN_AIRPORT_ID, ORIGIN_AIRPORT_SEQ_ID, ORIGIN_ CITY_MARKET_ID, ORIGIN, ORIGIN_STATE_ABR, DEST_AIRPORT_ID, DEST_AIRPORT_ SEQ_ID, DEST_CITY_MARKET_ID, DEST, DEST_STATE_ABR, DEP_TIME, DEP_DELAY, ARR_TIME, ARR_DELAY, CANCELLED, CANCELLATION_CODE, DIVERTED, AIR_TIME, DISTANCE, CARRIER_DELAY, WEATHER_DELAY, NAS_DELAY, SECURITY_DELAY, and LATE_AIRCRAFT_DELAY.

Additionally, we will download the lookup files.

This website downloads the files to your local directory. Rename the files to the following format T_ONTIME_YYYYMMDD.csv. The following table shows you the files required for the mini project:

File name/s	Description
/otp/stage/rawotp/T_ONTIME_201301.csv /otp/stage/rawotp/T_ONTIME_201406.csv	These files are the detailed on-time performance flight data for every flight organized by one file per year and month.
/otp/stage/lookup/airportcode.csv	This is a lookup file that has a full name for each airport abbreviation.
/otp/stage/lookup/cancellationcode.csv	This file has a full description of the cancellation abbreviation.
/otp/stage/lookup/dayofweek.csv	This file has a full description of the day of week.

Transferring to HDFS

Launch the Hadoop command line and use the following commands to upload the complete directory to HDFS:

```
C:\>hadoop fs -mkdir -p /otp/stage/rawotp

c:\> hadoop fs -put D:\Users\hdinduser2\Downloads\OTPData\stage\rawotp\ /
otp/stage/rawotp/

C:\>hadoop fs -mkdir -p /otp/stage/lookup

c:\>hadoop fs -put D:\Users\hdinduser2\Downloads\OTPData\stage\lookup\ /
otp/stage/lookup/
```

Loading data to Azure Blob storage using Azure PowerShell

Azure HDInsight provides 100 percent HDFS functionality using Azure Blob storage under the covers. So, to load data to the cluster, we can load data straight to Azure Blob storage without the need of the HDInsight cluster, thereby, making this more cost effective. In this section, we will see how to load data to Azure Blob using Azure PowerShell.

To load the data to Azure Blob storage from a local filesystem, we will perform the following steps:

1. Open Azure PowerShell using the shortcut on your desktop and type in the `Get-AzurePublishSettingsFile` command. This will open the `manage.windowsazure.com` web page and download a `.publishsettings` file.

2. Next, type in the `Import-AzurePublishSettingsFile` command with the `publishsettings` file to import the management certificate.

3. If you have multiple Azure subscriptions, you will need to use the `Set-AzureSubscription` command to the context of PowerShell:

   ```
   Set-AzureSubscription -SubscriptionName "Pay-As-You-Go"
   ```

4. Next, set the storage account name, container name, get the storage key, and set the storage context:

   ```
   $storageAccountName = "hdindstorage"

   $containerName = "hdind"

   $storageAccountKey = Get-AzureStorageKey $storageAccountName |
   %{$_ .Primary}
   ```

```
$storageContext = New-AzureStorageContext -StorageAccountName
$storageAccountName -StorageAccountKey $storageAccountKey
```

 Make sure that the container already exists; otherwise you will get an error.

5. Next, set the variables for the local filename and Blob location in Azure:

```
$fileName = "Z:\HDInsightver2\OTPData\otp\stage\rawotp\T_
ONTIME_201201.csv"

$blobName = "otp/stage/rawotp/T_ONTIME_201201.csv"
```

6. Finally, upload the file using the `Set-AzureStorageBlobContent` command, as follows:

```
Set-AzureStorageBlobContent -File $fileName -Container
$containerName -Blob $blobName -context $storageContext
```

With the preceding steps, we have successfully loaded the local file `Z:\HDInsightver2\OTPData\otp\stage\rawotp\T_ONTIME_201201.csv` to the Azure Blob `otp/stage/rawotp/T_ONTIME_201201.csv` in the `hdind` container.

The following screenshot shows you the results of the preceding commands:

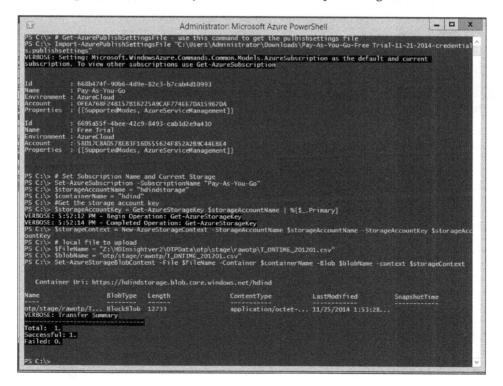

The preceding script can be tailored to automate the ingestion of data on a regular basis to the Data Lake.

Loading files to Data Lake using GUI tools

In this section, we will see how to load data to the cluster using graphical user interface tools.

Storage access keys

To use any of the Azure Blob storage explorer tools, you will need your storage access keys. For instructions, you can refer to *Chapter 4, Administering Your HDInsight Cluster*.

Storage tools

There are several tools that you can use to load data to the Azure Storage; some of them are freeware. I have listed the popular ones here and will show you CloudXplorer in detail:

- CloudXplorer: `http://clumsyleaf.com/products/cloudxplorer`
- Azure Storage Explorer: `http://azurestorageexplorer.codeplex.com/`
- Azure Management Studio: `http://www.cerebrata.com/products/azure-management-studio/introduction`
- CloudBerry Explorer: `http://www.cloudberrylab.com/microsoft-azure-explorer-pro.aspx`

CloudXplorer

CloudXplorer is a simple GUI tool that allows you to browse, upload, and delete blobs in Azure Storage. It has a simple Windows Explorer-like interface and supports multiple Windows Azure storage accounts.

Key benefits

The following are the key benefits of using a tool such as CloudXplorer:

- CloudXplorer user interface is very intuitive and easy to use Windows File Explorer
- It supports upload of multiple files and directories with the option to run parallel threads
- It supports restart of failed uploads
- It supports copy and move operations between folders, containers, and even accounts

Let's explore this in detail. First, download and install software from `http://clumsyleaf.com/products/cloudxplorer`.

Registering your storage account

After installation, you will need to register the Azure storage account used for HDInsight with CloudXplorer. Perform the following steps:

1. Click on **Manage Accounts**.
2. Select **Azure Blobs account**.
3. Enter a storage name and the storage key, as obtained from the Azure portal.

The following screenshot shows you the preceding steps:

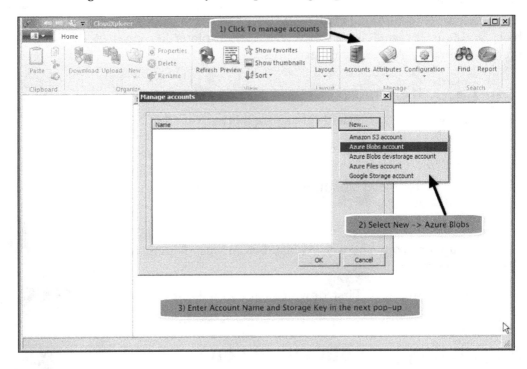

Uploading files to your Blob storage

Next, perform the following steps to upload local files as Azure blobs:

1. Browse to the desired storage container and directory.(You can also add new directories by clicking on the **New** icon next to **Upload**.)

2. Click on the **Upload** icon on the menu bar.

3. Select the file/s you want to be uploaded and click on **Open**.

4. This will start the upload to the Azure storage in the cloud.

5. Optionally, you can change the preferences to run multiple upload threads in parallel.

6. Once the upload is complete, you can verify the files by viewing the list in the directory that you uploaded.

The following screenshot shows you the preceding steps:

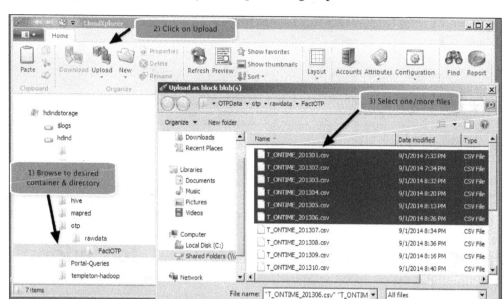

With the preceding steps, we have uploaded the six `.csv` files to Azure Blob storage using CloudXplorer.

Using Sqoop to move data from RDBMS to Data Lake

Sqoop enables us to transfer data between any relational database and Hadoop. You can import data from any relational database that has a JDBC adaptor such as SQL Server, MySQL, Oracle, Teradata, and others, to HDInsight.

Key benefits

The major benefits of using Sqoop to move data are as follows:

- Leverages RDBMS metadata to get the column data types
- It is simple to script and uses SQL
- It can be used to handle change data capture by importing daily transactional data to HDInsight
- It uses MapReduce for export and import that enables parallel and efficient data movement

Two modes of using Sqoop

Sqoop can be used to get data into and out of Hadoop; it has two modes of operation:

- **Sqoop import**: Data moves from RDBMS to HDInsight
- **Sqoop export**: Data moves from HDInsight to RDBMS

The following screenshot shows you two modes of using Sqoop:

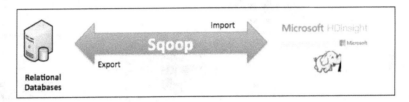

Using Sqoop to import data (SQL to Hadoop)

The following is the setup for a Sqoop import demonstration:

- Source database: Teradata
- Server: 10.11.12.6
- SQL username: dbc
- SQL Password: dbc123
- Table: `airline_otp` (has 509,519 rows)
- Target: `/user/rajn/TDStage2`

The following are the steps to import data using Sqoop:

1. Ensure that you have necessary JDBC drivers. Copy them to the Sqoop `lib` folder. In my installation, it was `C:\Hadoop\sqoop-1.4.2\lib`. I copied `terajdbc4.jar` and `tdgssconfig.jar`.

> A prerequisite for Sqoop to work is that connectivity to the SQL database should be available that requires proper ports and firewall settings so that the HDInsight cluster can communicate with the database server.

2. Use Windows PowerShell and run the Sqoop `import` command:

```
C:\Hadoop\sqoop-1.4.2\bin> .\sqoop import --connect
"jdbc:teradata://10.11.12.6" --username dbc --password dbc123
--table "airline_otp" --driver com.teradata.jdbc.TeraDriver
--target-dir /user/rajn/TDStage2 -m 1
```

`-m 1` ensures that there is only one map task and hence one file that has a complete dataset.

3. Verify the data in HDFS using a `tail` command:

```
c:\Hadoop\sqoop-1.4.2\lib>hadoop fs -tail  /user/rajn/TDStage2/
part-m-00000
```

4. You can optionally filter the data using a where clause. For the preceding dataset, let's filter for flights where carrier is AA (American Airlines):

```
C:\Hadoop\sqoop-1.4.2\bin> .\sqoop import --connect
"jdbc:teradata://10.11.12.6" --username dbc --password dbc --table
"airline_otp" --driver com.teradata.jdbc.TeraDriver --target-dir /
user/rajn/TDStage3 --where " uniquecarrier='AA' " -m 1
```

Sqoop can also be used to export data out from Hadoop and send it to RDBMS. For details, refer to the Sqoop User Guide. The link to the user guide is available at `http://sqoop.apache.org/docs/1.4.4/SqoopUserGuide.html#_literal_sqoop_export_literal`.

Organizing your Data Lake in HDFS

As you load files to your Data Lake, it is important to have this process managed for data consumers in order to find the right data. Organization of data requires planning, coordination, and governance. One proposed model that I have seen used by several clients is to have three main directories:

- **Staging**: This directory will host all the original source files, as they get ingested to the Data Lake. Each source should have its own directory. For example, let's consider that an organization has two financial databases, `findb01` and `findb02`. A proposed directory structure in Data Lake can be `/data/stage/findb01` and `/data/stage/findb02`.

- **Cleansed**: The data in staging should go through basic audit and data quality checks to ensure that it meets the organization standards. For example, if sales data is being ingested to Data Lake, the state and country code in the sales records should be valid. The cleansed data should be grouped by subject area, for example, finance and sales. A proposed directory structure for the cleansed data is `data/cleansed/finance`.

- **Summarized**: Data that is often used by reports should be precomputed for performance and this is called summarized data. For example, a regular report required for an enterprise is quarterly profitability and forecast by country, region, and state, which requires data from sales and finance to be summarized. A proposed directory structure for summarized data is `data/summary/findw`.

To keep a track of which file is in which directory, it is recommended that you index all this information into a search index such as Elastic search or SOLR. The following is the recommended information for such an index: date of ingestion, filename, source information, destination, file size, and additional attributes that is known about the file. This can be accomplished by a scheduled Oozie workflow that scans the data files in HDFS and builds or updates the SOLR index.

The following figure shows you the data flow and the various directories in a managed Data Lake:

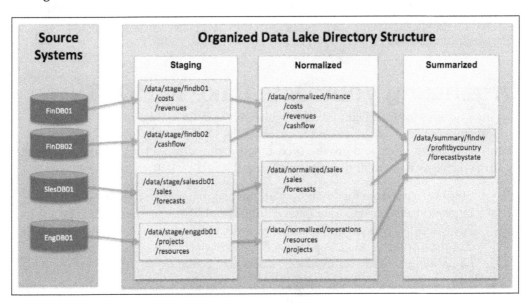

Managing file metadata using HCatalog

Organizing data in specific directories based on the content and source does provide the foundation for a well-managed Data Lake. In addition to file location, a managed Data Lake should capture key attributes and structure information of the file; for example, for the sales table being ingested to Data Lake in `data/stage/salesdb01/sales`, the attributes will be as follows:

- **Structure of the file**: For example, fixed length, delimited, XML, JSON, sequence, and columnar (RC)
- **Fields/columns in the data file**: For example, fiscal quarter, $amount
- **Data types of the fields**: For example, integer, string, double, and string

Apache HCatalog provides a table management system for the HDFS based filesystem. It provides the equivalent of `information_schema` tables of SQL Server. HCatalog will store the format/structure information.

Key benefits

The following are the key benefits of using HCatalog:

- Stores structural metadata of HDFS files in a shared metastore
- Provides interface to metastore for various Hadoop tools such as Pig, Hive, and MapReduce
- Provides table abstraction so that users don't have to worry about where and how data is stored in the Data Lake
- Provides APIs and command-line tools to interact with HCatalog metadata

The following figure shows the architecture of HCatalog and Hadoop ecosystem tools:

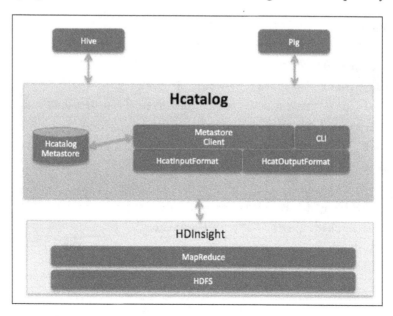

Using HCatalog Command Line to create tables

HCatalog Command Line is a convenient way to register metadata with HCatalog. Let's review how this can be done for our OTP datasets that we ingested to Hadoop.

First, we will build an HCatalog script that has four `create table` commands for the OTP data and the lookups. We will create these tables as *external* tables, which means that the data files are retained in their original directory and HCatalog only references the location.

Let's review the `create table` commands that you can save as a `otpcreatetable.sql.txt` file:

```
-- Create Database
create database otpdw;


use otpdw;


-- Create stage table for OTP data
CREATE EXTERNAL TABLE airline_otp_stage (
    flightyear        SMALLINT,   -- Year
    flightquarter     SMALLINT,   -- Quarter
    flightmonth       SMALLINT,   -- Month
    flightdayofmonth SMALLINT,    -- Day of Month
    flightdayofweek   SMALLINT,   -- Day of week
    flightdate        STRING,      -- Flight Date (yyyy-mm-dd)
    uniquecarrier     STRING,      -- Unique Carrier Code.
    airlineid         INT,         -- Identification number carrier
    flightnum         STRING,      -- Flight Number
    originairportid INT,           -- Origin Airport,
    originaiportseqid INT,      -- Airport Seq ID
    origincitymarketid INT, --      CityMarketID
    originairportabr         STRING,   -- Origin airport ABR
    origincityname          STRING, -- Origin city name
    originstateabr          STRING,   -- Origin State ABR
    destairportid INT,           -- Origin Airport,
    destaiportseqid INT,      -- Airport Seq ID
    destcitymarketid INT, --      CityMarketID
```

```
    destairportabr         STRING,   -- Origin airport ABR
    destcityname          STRING,  -- Origin city name
    deststateabr          STRING,   -- Origin State ABR
    deptime            STRING,      -- Actual Departure Time (hhmm)
    depdelay           STRING,      -- Difference in minutes
    arrtime            STRING,      -- Actual Arrival Time (hhmm)
    arrdelay           STRING,      -- Difference in minutes
    cancelled          STRING,      -- (1=Yes) -> true/false 0.00
    cancelcode         STRING,      -- Cancelation code null
    diverted           STRING,      -- (1=Yes) -> true/false
    airtime            DOUBLE,      -- Airtime in minutes
    distance           DOUBLE,      -- Distance in miles
    carrierdelay       STRING,      -- delay due to carrier
    weatherdelay       STRING,      -- delay due to weather
    nasdelay           STRING,      -- delay due to nas
    securitydelay      STRING,      -- delay due to security
    lateaircraftdelay STRING       -- delay due to late aircraft
)
row format DELIMITED
fields terminated by ','
LOCATION '/otp/stage/rawotp';


-- airport code
CREATE EXTERNAL TABLE airport_code_stage (
    aiportcode             STRING,  -- Origin airport abr "DFW"
    airportdescription    STRING  -- description of airport
 )
row format DELIMITED
fields terminated by ','
LOCATION '/otp/stage/lookup/airportcode';


-- cancellation code
CREATE EXTERNAL TABLE cancellation_code_stage (
    cancellationcode           STRING,  -- Cancel code like A
    cancellationdescription    STRING  -- description like Carrier
 )
```

```
row format DELIMITED
fields terminated by ','
LOCATION '/otp/stage/lookup/cancellationcode';


-- Dayofweek code
CREATE EXTERNAL TABLE dayofweek_code_stage (
    dayofweekcode             STRING,   -- Cancel code like A
    dayofweekcodedescription  STRING  -- description like Carrier
 )
row format DELIMITED
fields terminated by ','
LOCATION '/otp/stage/lookup/dayofweekcode';
```

Next, we will call the script via the HCatalog command-line interface. Let's perform the following steps to do so:

1. Log in to the head node of the HDInsight cluster using the remote desktop.

2. Launch the Hadoop Command Line executable.

3. Perform the following commands that will call HCatalog and run the `create table` commands:

   ```
   c:\> cd C:\apps\dist\hive-0.13.0.2.1.5.0-2057\hcatalog\bin

   C:\apps\dist\hive-0.13.0.2.1.5.0-2057\hcatalog\bin>hcat.py -f D:\
   Users\hdinduser2\Downloads\otpcreatetable.sql
   ```

After the preceding command is run, the four tables are registered and visible in HCatalog and Hive.

Summary

An Enterprise Data Lake journey starts first with getting valuable data into the lake. There are several mechanisms to ingest data into a Data Lake powered by HDInsight primarily: HDFS transfer, Azure PowerShell, Azure tools with a user interface, and Sqoop. In order to make a Data Lake easy to consume, it is important to have a managed ingestion process with governance and structure of the various directories.

HCatalog provides a shared metastore that can be used by various tools in Hadoop, namely, Hive, Pig, and MapReduce. This ensures that the structural information is defined once and leveraged by these tools. In the next chapter, we will look into the transformation of the data that we just ingested.

6
Transform Data in the Data Lake

In the previous chapter, we ingested the source data into the Data Lake. To make sense of the vast amount of raw data, a transformation procedure is required to convert it into information that can further be used by decision makers. In this chapter, we will discuss how to transform data.

The topics covered in this chapter are as follows:

- Transformation overview
- Tools for transforming data in a Data Lake, such as HCatalog, Hive, Pig, and MapReduce
- Transformation of the airline **on-time performance** (OTP) raw data into an aggregate
- Review results of transformation

Transformation overview

Once you get data into the cluster, the next step in a typical project is to get data ready for future consumption. This typically involves data cleaning, data quality, and aggregation; for example, checking phone number format, valid date of birth, and aggregate sales by region.

In our mini project case, we are in step two of the data pipeline to the Data Lake.

Tools for transforming data in Data Lake

In this section, we will review the various tools that enable the transformation of data in the Data Lake. We will review HCatalog, Hive, and Pig in detail, which are the popular methods to transform data in Data Lake. Next, we will look at how Azure PowerShell enables easy assembly of these scripts into a single procedure.

HCatalog

Apache HCatalog manages metadata of the structure of files in Hadoop. In *Chapter 5, Ingest and Organize Data Lake*, we registered stage tables with HCatalog, and in this chapter, we will leverage that information for transformation.

Persisting HCatalog metastore in a SQL database

With Azure HDInsight, the metastore can be hosted in an embedded mode in Apache Derby, which comes with the standard Hadoop. However, one issue with this approach is that every time you shut down HDInsight, the metastore information is lost. An alternative is to store HCatalog information in a separately managed SQL database. Perform the following steps for this:

1. Create a new Azure SQL database using the Azure management page. For the demo project, I have selected the following database settings:
    ◦ **NAME**: HdindHcatalogDB
    ◦ **SERVICE TIERS**: Basic
    ◦ **MAXIMUM SIZE**: 2 GB
    ◦ **REGION**: West US (same as the HDInsight cluster)

2. When you bring up the HDInsight cluster, check the **Enter the Hive/ Oozie Metastore** option, and select the newly created metastore database `HdindHcatalogDB`:

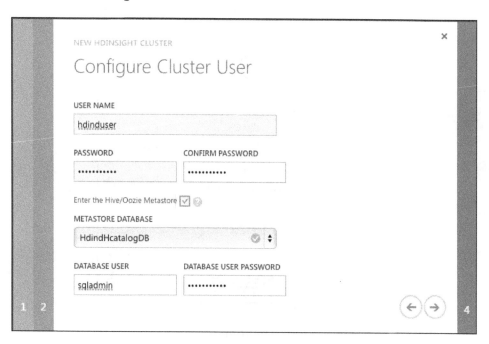

Apache Hive

Apache Hive is a data warehouse infrastructure built on top of Hadoop and provides easy querying, summarization, and analysis. Facebook engineers initially developed Hive to help their business users to be effective in accessing the Data Lake without the need of complex programming skills. Hive comes with HiveQL, which is a simple SQL-like language, that allows queries to be compiled to MapReduce and then runs on the cluster.

Hive architecture

A high-level Hive architecture is shown in the following figure:

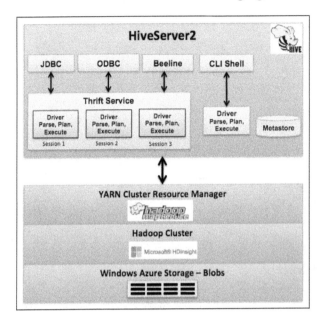

Let's view the architecture from top to bottom:

- Hive can be accessed via JDBC, ODBC, Beeline, and a **command-line interface (CLI)**.
- CLI communicates directly with a driver that will parse, plan, and execute the queries provided by the user. CLI requires Hadoop and Hive client.
- A modern way to connect to Hive is using Beeline, which is lightweight and requires only a JDBC driver. JDBC, Beeline, and ODBC all communicate with the Thrift service, which has a session manager, and can execute multiple Hive commands at the same time using separate drivers.
- Hive driver converts the HiveQL to a MapReduce task and submits it to the Hadoop cluster.
- Metastore is typically a relational database and has the structure information of the files.

 Since Hive is based on Hadoop, it will not support `update`, `delete`, and row-level `insert` statements.

Starting Hive in HDInsight

To launch Hive, perform the following steps:

1. Connect to your head node and then click on the Hadoop Command Line icon on your desktop.

2. Next, change the directory to Hive home and then type the word `hive`.

3. Once you get Command Prompt, just type `hive`. This will start the Hive session ready for Hive commands. It is recommended that you first create a separate database for each application.

The following code snippet shows you the commands to start a Hive session:

```
C:\> cd C:\apps\dist\hive-0.13.0.2.1.5.0-2057\bin
C:\apps\dist\hive-0.13.0.2.1.5.0-2057\bin> hive
```

Basic Hive commands

The following table shows you the commonly used Hive commands with examples:

Syntax	Description
`hive -f   C:\Downloads\emp.sql`	This command launches Hive with a filename `emp.sql`.
`create database otpdw;`	This command creates a database named `otpdw`.

`CREATE TABLE employees (name STRING, salary FLOAT, subordinates ARRAY<STRING>, address STRING ) PARTITIONED BY (deptno STRING)`
 	
`ROW FORMAT DELIMITED FIELDS TERMINATED BY '\t'`
 	
`STORED AS TEXTFILE;`
	This command creates the `employees` table with four columns partitioned by department and is stored as a text file.

`Describe employees;`	This command describes the structure of the `employees` table.
`LOAD DATA LOCAL INPATH '/training/demo/data' OVERWRITE INTO TABLE demo;`	This command loads data into a table `demo` from data in HDFS.
`INSERT OVERWRITE TABLE demonames PARTITION(place='US') select firstname, lastname from demo where country='US';`	This command inserts into table `demonames` with select operation on another table called `demo`.
`Drop table employees;`	This command drops the `employees` table.

Syntax	Description
`SELECT e.name, e.joinyear, d.dname FROM employees e LEFT OUTER JOIN department d ON (e.deptno = d.deptid);`	This command selects `employees` and `department` tables with a join.
`INSERT OVERWRITE LOCAL DIRECTORY '/usr/rajn/employeesafter2000' select id, name, salary from employees where id > 2000;`	This command exports data into the local filesystem from the `employees` table with a filter on the employees with ID greater than 2000.

Apache Pig

Apache Pig is another high-level language for processing data in Hadoop and was developed by the Yahoo engineering team. It provides a simple scripting language that is similar to Python and simplifies joining data and chaining sets of operations. Pig scripts are converted to MapReduce and submitted to the cluster.

The key features of Pig are as follows:

- Pig allows rapid prototyping of algorithms
- Iterative processing of data (chaining)
- Joins are easy using Pig to correlate datasets
- Data can be verified on screen or saved back to HDFS

Pig architecture

The following figure shows you the Pig architecture:

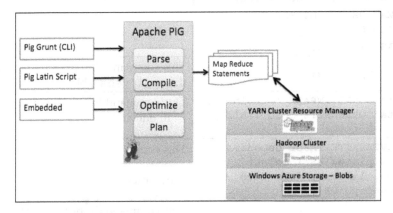

Let's view the architecture from left to right:

- Access to Pig can be via a CLI called Grunt, Pig script, or an embedded program such as Java
- Pig parses, compiles, optimizes, and fires MapReduce statements
- MapReduce accesses HDFS and returns the results

Starting Pig in HDInsight node

To launch Pig, perform the following steps:

1. Connect to your head node and then click on the Hadoop Command Line icon on your desktop.
2. Next, change the directory to Pig home and then type the word `pig`.
3. Now, this takes you to the Pig grunt command line that is ready to take in Pig commands.

   The following snippet shows you the commands to start a Pig grunt session:

   ```
   C:\> cd C:\apps\dist\pig-0.12.1.2.1.5.0-2057\bin
   C:\apps\dist\pig-0.12.1.2.1.5.0-2057\bin>pig
   ```

Basic Pig commands

The following table shows you the commonly used Pig commands with examples:

Syntax	Description
`pig -useHCatalog D:\Downloads\Cleanotpraw.pig.txt`	This command launches Pig with HCatalog integration.
`users = LOAD '/u01/c01/users' USING PigStorage('\t')` `AS (name:chararray, id:int, email:chararray);`	This command selects all users from a file.
`userswithnewids = FILTER users BY id > 20;`	This command filters users whose ID is greater than 20.
`names = FOREACH users GENERATE name;` `distinctnames = DISTINCT names;`	This command gets distinct user names.
`EMPDEPT = JOIN EMP BY $0, DEPT BY $1;`	This command join results from EMP and DEPT to create a combined EMPDEPT dataset.

Syntax	Description
`DUMP names;`	This command dumps results on the standard output.
`STORE names INTO '/pigoutput/employees';`	This command stores results to a file in HDFS.

 DUMP and STORE are trigger words for Pig; only after these words, will Pig start the execution of all the statements preceding that line.

Pig or Hive

If you have a question whether to use Pig or Hive, think of a pipeline of ETL operations from raw data in HDFS to a BI analytical user. Pig can be used for doing core ETL where the algorithms are known and Hive can be used for ad hoc queries.

The following figure shows you a recommended data pipeline from ingestion to HDFS to query using Hive:

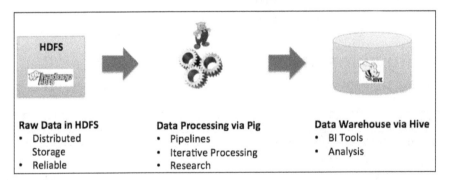

MapReduce

MapReduce is another option for batch data transformation and requires Java programming skills. In this section, we will look at the basic wordcount problem solution using MapReduce. The goal of this code is to count the unique words in a text file.

 This wordcount is a common MapReduce example and is also explained in the Azure webpage at http://azure.microsoft.com/en-us/documentation/articles/hdinsight-use-mapreduce/.

The mapper code

The following is the mapper side of the code that reads every line of the text file and outputs a key value for every word in the line where key is the word and value is set to "1". For example, if the line is "This is my first line in this file", the mapper will emit the following output:

```
This:1       is:1       my:1       first:1      line:1
in:1         this:1     file:1
```

The content of WordCountMapper.java is as follows:

```
public class WordCountMapper extends Mapper<Object, Text, Text,
IntWritable> {

   private Text word = new Text();
   private final static IntWritable ONE = new IntWritable(1);
      public void map(Object key, Text value, Context context)
         throws IOException, InterruptedException {

      // Break line into words for processing
      StringTokenizer wordList = new StringTokenizer(value.toString());

      while (wordList.hasMoreTokens()) {
        word.set(wordList.nextToken());
        context.write(word, ONE);
      }
   }
}
```

The reducer code

The following is the reducer side of the code that gets the input from the mapper and aggregates the words. In our example, the reducer will emit the following output:

```
This:2       is:1       my:1      first:1     line:1     in:1     file:1
```

The content of WordCountReducer.java is as follows:

```
public class WordCountReducer extends Reducer<Text, IntWritable, Text,
IntWritable> {

   private IntWritable totalWordCount = new IntWritable();
   public void reduce(Text key, Iterable<IntWritable> values, Context
context)
         throws IOException, InterruptedException {
```

```
    int wordCount = 0;
    for (IntWritable val : values) {
      wordCount += val.get();
    }

    totalWordCount.set(wordCount);
    context.write(key, totalWordCount);
  }
}
```

The driver code

To execute the mapper and reducer, we need a driver, which is as shown in the following snippet.

The content of the WordCount.java snippet is as follows:

```
public class WordCount {

  public static void main(String[] args) throws Exception {
    if (args.length != 2) {
      System.out.println("Usage: WordCount <input dir> <output dir>");
      System.exit(-1);
    }

    Job job = new Job();
    job.setJarByClass(WordCount.class);
    job.setJobName("WordCount");
    FileInputFormat.addInputPath(job, new Path(args[0]));
    FileOutputFormat.setOutputPath(job, new Path(args[1]));
    job.setMapperClass(WordCountMapper.class);
    job.setReducerClass(WordCountReducer.class);
    job.setOutputKeyClass(Text.class);
    job.setOutputValueClass(IntWritable.class);
    System.exit(job.waitForCompletion(true) ? 0 : 1);
  }
}
```

Executing MapReduce on HDInsight

Now, we are ready to use the MapReduce code to get the frequency of words in the data file. Let's perform the following steps:

1. Connect to your head node and then click on the Hadoop Command Line icon on your desktop.

2. Next, you can invoke the MapReduce code using the following command:

   ```
   hadoop jar hadoop-mapreduce.jar wordcount input output
   ```

   Here, the `hadoop-mapreduce.jar` is a sample MapReduce.jar provided by HDInsight. There are two arguments for the MapReduce job, first is the source filename and second is the output file path.

3. Once the MapReduce job is complete, the output file/s will be created in the location as specified. The default name for the output file for a MapReduce job is `part-r-00000`. If the result has more than one reducer, additional files will be created and named `part-r-00001`, `part-r-00002`, and so on.

4. You can view the contents of the file using the `hadoop fs -cat outputfilename` command.

The following command performs the word count for a text file called `Nasa_Human_Spaceflight_Report` and creates an output file in the directory `NasaWordCountOutput`:

```
C:\Users\rajn\SampleCode\WordCount>hadoop jar hadoop-mapreduce.jar
wordcount /user/hadoop/wcount/Nasa_Human_Spaceflight_Report.txt /user/
hadoop/wcount/NasaWordCountOutput
```

Azure PowerShell for execution of Hadoop jobs

Azure PowerShell is a powerful scripting environment that allows one to submit Hive, Pig, MapReduce, and Sqoop jobs to the HDInsight cluster. The following script shows you how to execute a Hive query using Azure PowerShell. The script can be extended to call a Pig or MapReduce code as well:

```
#Import azure credentials

Get-AzurePublishSettingsFile

Import-AzurePublishSettingsFile "C:\Users\Rajesh Nadipalli\Downloads\Pay-As-You-Go-Free Trial-9-15-2014-credentials.publishsettings"

#Set Subscription

Select-AzureSubscription "Pay-As-You-Go"


# Define Hive Query

$queryString = "CREATE TABLE demo_table (id int, name string);; "
```

```
# Use the HDInsight cmdlet to create a HDInsight job definition, with the
HiveQL

$hiveJobDefinition = New-AzureHDInsightHiveJobDefinition -Query
$queryString


# Start the HDInsight job using the Hive job definition

$hiveJob = Start-AzureHDInsightJob -Cluster $clusterName -JobDefinition $
hiveJobDefinition
```

Transformation for the OTP project

Let's take a look at a practical example of a transformation using our **Airline Ontime Performance (OTP)** project. Let's say that our transformation task is to get from a source stage table that we created in *Chapter 5, Ingest and Organize Data Lake*, (which is on the left-hand side) to aggregated (which is on the right-hand side) summary data by airline carrier, year, and month.

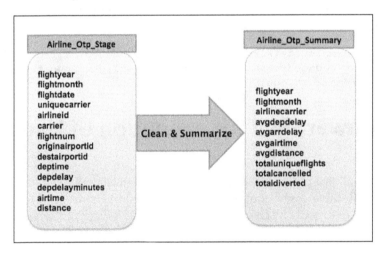

To achieve the preceding transformation, we need to perform the following key steps:

1. Clean the header line in each file that has the field names.
2. Update the flight month from the current "MM" to "YYYYMM" format.
3. Create an intermediate table with the refined data from the previous two steps.
4. Aggregate the data from the refined data to a summary table at flight year, flight month, and carrier levels.

We will use Pig to do a cleanup and then use Hive to preserve the results as shown in the following figure:

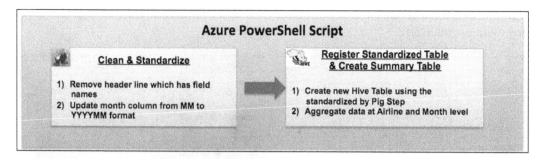

Cleaning data using Pig

The following is a Pig script (saved as `Cleanotpraw.pig.txt`) that will perform the following steps:

1. Read structure information from HCatalog.

2. Remove the header line.

3. Change the flight date to YYYMM format.

 The following is a code snippet of the Pig code, the complete code is available for download from the publisher's website.

```
-- Load using Hcatalog table name
fileAllRows = LOAD 'otpdw.airline_otp_stage' USING org.apache.
hcatalog.pig.HCatLoader();


-- remove the header lines
fileDataRows = FILTER fileAllRows BY NOT(originairportabr MATCHES
'.*ORIGIN.*');


-- concat YYYYMM to form the new flightmonth
fileDataStandardized = FOREACH fileDataRows GENERATE
flightyear, flightquarter, CONCAT(SUBSTRING(flightdate, 0,
4),SUBSTRING(flightdate, 5, 7)) as flightmonth...
```

Executing Pig script

To execute the Pig script, connect to your head node and then click on the Hadoop Command Line icon on your desktop and type the command highlighted in the following screenshot:

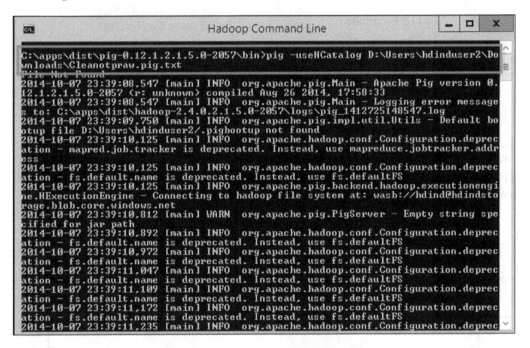

Registering a refined and aggregate table using Hive

After Pig standardizes the data, the following Hive script will first create a Hive table on top of the refined data and then create an aggregate table with the desired results.

The following are the key steps in the Hive scripts:

1. Create an external hive table `airline_otp_refined` on top of the data produced by the previous Pig script.

An external table in Hive can point to any location in HDFS rather than the regular table that is stored in the directory, as specified in the Hive configuration file (`hive.metastore.warehouse.dir`).

2. Create a new summary table `airline_otp_summary`.

3. Insert into `airline_otp_summary` using data from `airline_otp_refined`.

The following is the Hive script that will create the `airline_otp_summary` table using the data refined by Pig in the previous step:

```
use otpdw;
CREATE EXTERNAL TABLE airline_otp_refined (
    flightyear       SMALLINT,   -- Year
    flightquarter    SMALLINT,   -- Quarter
    flightmonth      STRING,    -- Month in YYYYMM format
    flightdayofmonth SMALLINT,  -- Day of Month
    flightdayofweek  SMALLINT,  -- Day of week
    flightdate       STRING,    -- Flight Date (yyyy-mm-dd)
    uniquecarrier    STRING,    -- Unique Carrier Code.    "9E"
    airlineid        INT,   -- Identification number for carrier
    flightnum        STRING,    -- Flight Number   3324
    originairportid INT,        -- Origin Airport,   11298
    originaiportseqid INT,    -- Airport Seq ID   1129803
    origincitymarketid INT, --    CityMarketID 30194
    originairportabr     STRING,   -- Origin airport abr "DFW"
    originstateabr       STRING,   -- Origin State ABR "TX"
    destairportid INT,          -- Origin Airport,   12478
    destaiportseqid INT,     -- Airport Seq ID   1247802
    destcitymarketid INT, --     CityMarketID 31703
    destairportabr       STRING,   -- Origin airport abr "JFK"
    deststateabr         STRING,   -- Origin State ABR "NY"
    deptime          STRING,    -- Actual Departure Time (hhmm)   1038
    depdelay         STRING, -- Difference in minutes (minus is early)
    arrtime          STRING,    -- Actual Arrival Time (hhmm) 1451
    arrdelay         STRING,    -- Difference in minutes
    cancelled        STRING,    -- (1=Yes) -> true/false 0.00
    cancelcode       STRING,    -- Cancelation code null
    diverted         STRING,    -- (1=Yes) -> true/false 0.00
    airtime          DOUBLE,    -- Airtime in minutes 175.00
    distance         DOUBLE,    -- Distance in miles 1391.00
    carrierdelay     STRING,    -- delay in minutes due to carrier
```

```
        weatherdelay        STRING,      -- delay in minutes due to weather
        nasdelay            STRING,      -- delay in minutes due to nas
        securitydelay       STRING,      -- delay in minutes due to security
        lateaircraftdelay STRING         -- delay in min dueto late aircraft)
row format DELIMITED
fields terminated by ','
LOCATION '/otp/stage/refinedotp';


-- Now Aggregated table for summary
dfs -mkdir -p /otp/summary/airlinesumm;


create external table airline_otp_summary (
        flightyear          SMALLINT,  -- Year
        flightquarter       SMALLINT,  -- Quarter
        flightmonth         STRING,   -- Month in YYYYMM format
        airlinecarrier      STRING,     -- Unique Carrier Code."9E"
        avgdepdelay         DOUBLE,
        avgarrdelay         DOUBLE,
        totaluniqueflights DOUBLE,
        totalcancelled      DOUBLE,
        totaldiverted       DOUBLE,
        avgairtime          DOUBLE,
        avgdistance         DOUBLE)
row format DELIMITED
fields terminated by ','
LOCATION '/otp/summary/airlinesumm';


INSERT INTO TABLE airline_otp_summary
select flightyear, flightquarter, flightmonth ,
regexp_replace(uniquecarrier,"\"","") as airlinecarrier,
avg(depdelay) as avgdepdelay,
avg(arrdelay) as avgarrdelay,
count(distinct flightnum) as totaluniqueflights,
sum(cancelled) as totalcancelled,
sum(diverted) as totaldiverted,
avg(airtime) as avgairtime,
```

```
avg(distance) as avgdistance
from airline_otp_refined
group by flightyear, flightquarter, flightmonth ,
regexp_replace(uniquecarrier,"\"","");
```

Executing Hive script

To execute the Hive script, connect to your head node and then click on the Hadoop Command Line icon on your desktop and type the command highlighted in the following screenshot:

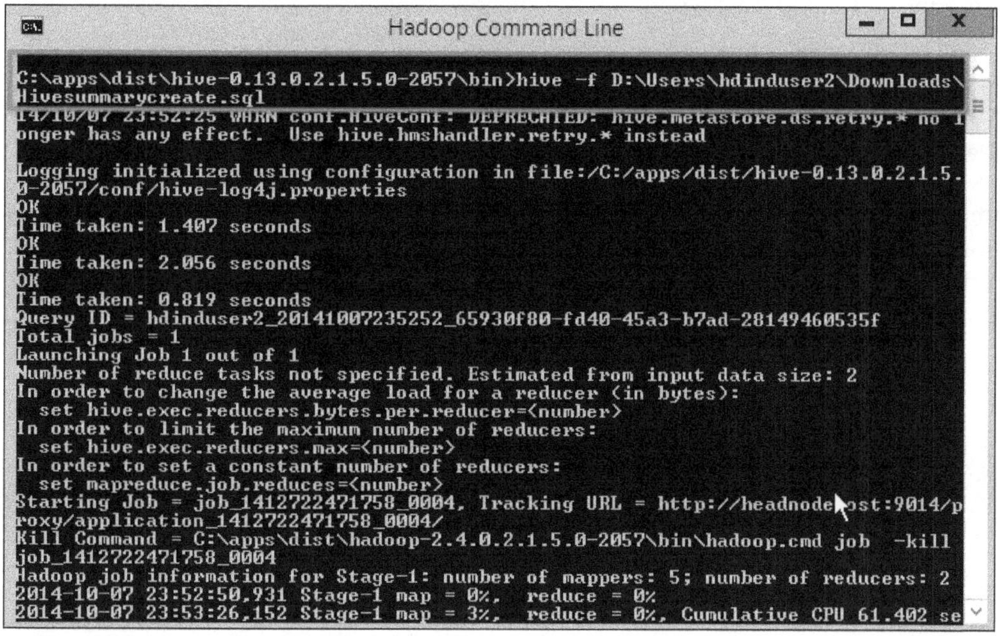

Reviewing results

Let's review the results from the transformation scripts that we created. The easiest way is to query the summary table in Hive as shown in the following command:

```
hive> select * from airline_otp_summary where flightmonth=201402;
```

Other tools used for transformation

The following are the other tools that should be considered when designing a transformation solution for HDInsight based on Data Lake.

Oozie

Oozie allows creation and scheduling of workflows in order to manage and orchestrate Apache Hadoop workloads such as Pig, MapReduce, and Hive programs. Workflows are defined in XML and submitted to the Oozie orchestration engine, which executes on the HDInsight cluster. Oozie workflows can be monitored using the command line, web interface, or PowerShell.

Spark

Spark is an open source processing engine for Hadoop data and designed for speed, ease of use, and sophisticated analytics. It claims to run Hadoop MapReduce 100 times faster in memory and 10 times faster even when running on disk. It is gaining momentum in the Hadoop ecosystem due to the performance and flexibility. Spark applications can be written in Java, Scala or Python, or using Spark SQL, which is compatible with HiveQL. Spark can run as a YARN application there by leveraging the power of the HDInsight cluster for the actual execution.

 As of December 2014, HDInsight does not support Spark but it is expected to be available in near future.

Summary

With every Data Lake initiative, over 50 percent of the project time is spent in transforming the data from its raw format to something that can be consumed by the decision makers. In this chapter, we looked at the key tools available for data transformation; Hive and Pig both provide a layer of abstraction over MapReduce and are easy for business users to adopt. Pig has a scripting interface and Hive has a SQL interface. Azure PowerShell provides the capability to orchestrate these various jobs in a sequence. In the next chapter, we will review how to utilize and visualize the data generated by this transformed process.

7
Analyze and Report from Data Lake

The real value of big data is when data becomes information that decision makers can take action with. In this chapter, we will review how to access data from Data Lake for analysis and reporting. The topics covered in this chapter are as follows:

- Data access overview
- Analysis using Excel and Microsoft Hive ODBC Driver
- Analysis using Excel Power Query
- Other business intelligence features in Excel
- Hive for ad hoc queries
- Other alternatives for analysis

Data access overview

Once we have data in a normalized and aggregated form, business analysts can run pivot tables and what-if analysis, and data scientists can run statistical analysis to present insights to executive management empowering them to make business decisions. This process of democratizing the Data Lake is also termed **Data access**.

For our airline on-time performance project in this chapter, we will analyze the aggregated and cleansed data that was performed in the previous chapter. The following figure shows the flow of data from **Ingest** to **Report**:

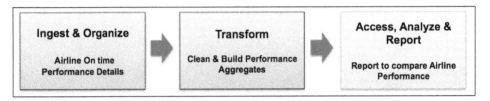

In the next few sections, we will see how to use Excel and other tools to perform analysis.

Analysis using Excel and Microsoft Hive ODBC driver

Excel is the most popular data analysis tool used by business analysts and now HDInsight makes it easy to integrate Excel with Hadoop using Hive. In this section, we will see how to use Excel against the data that is in our Data Lake using Hive.

Prerequisites

The prerequisites required are listed as follows:

- Office 2013 Professional Plus, Office 365 Pro Plus, Excel 2013 Standalone, or Office 2010 Professional plus
- Operating systems that are supported are Windows 7, Windows 8, Windows Server 2008 R2, or Windows Server 2012

The following are the steps to get your data into Excel and analyze it.

Step 1 – installing the Microsoft Hive ODBC driver

The first step is to download the Hive ODBC driver and set it up. Download the Hive ODBC driver from Microsoft Download Center based on your office version (2013 or 2010); the link for 2013 is `http://www.microsoft.com/en-us/download/details.aspx?id=40886`.

Once you download the driver MSI file to your local machine, double-click on it to install the driver. At the end of the installation, you will get a success confirmation message.

 There are two versions of the installation package: 32 bit or 64 bit. You should install the version that matches your office installation.

Step 2 – creating Hive ODBC Data Source

The next step is to configure Hive ODBC Data Source. Perform the following steps to create your Hive OBDC Data Source:

1. Navigate to **Start | Control Panel**.

2. Then, navigate to **System and Security | Administration tools**.

3. Next, click on **ODBC Data Sources** and select the user DSN.

4. Then, click on **Add**; this will enable you to add a new data source. Select Microsoft Hive ODBC Driver and click on **Finish**.

5. You will now see a **Microsoft Hive ODBC Driver DSN Setup** pop up. You will need to enter the following information:

    ° **Data Source Name**: Provide a name such as hdindhive.

    ° **Description**: Provide a description.

    ° **Host**: Provide a complete cluster name such as hdind. azurehdinsight.net for the Azure HDInsight service.

    ° **Port**: Use default 443. This is the port of the thrift server.

    ° **Hive Server Type**: Select **Hive Server 2**.

    ° **Mechanism**: Select **Windows Azure HDInsight Service**.

    ° **User Name** and **Password**: Enter the HDInsight cluster username and password.

The following screenshot shows a new Microsoft Hive ODBC Driver DSN configuration:

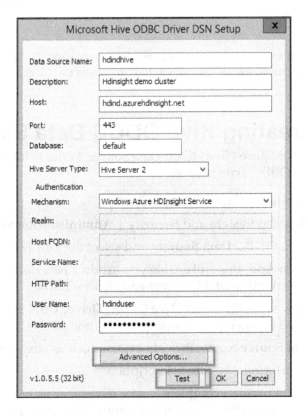

6. Next, click on the **Advanced Options...** tab to confirm certain parameters that impact the performance:

   ○ **Use Native Query**: Enable this if you are going to use HiveQL only

   ○ **Rows fetched per block**: When fetching large amounts of data, this parameter will help you optimize the performance

The following screenshot shows you the advanced options that are worth looking into for the Microsoft Hive ODBC Driver DSN configuration:

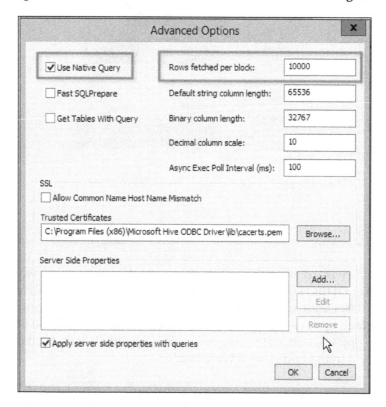

7. Next, click on **OK** and you will be back to the first tab of the ODBC configuration. Click on the **Test** button and verify the connection. You should receive a success message to proceed to the next step.

Step 3 – importing data to Excel

Once you have the new Hive data source set up, you can use Excel to analyze and visualize your data by performing the following steps:

1. Open a new Excel workbook and click on the **DATA** tab.

2. Click on **From Other Sources**.

3. Then, click on **From Data Connection Wizard**.

The following screenshot illustrates these steps:

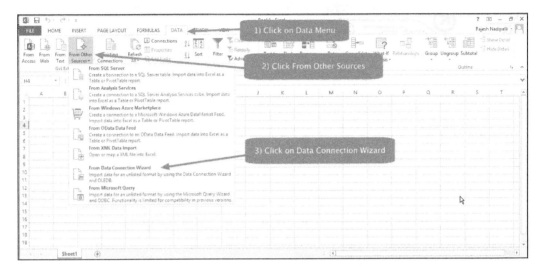

4. Next, the wizard will ask you which remote data source you want to connect to; select **ODBC DSN**. The next pop up should show you Microsoft Hive ODBC Data Source that you have just created, **hdindhive**. Continue with the default options till you see the **Select Database and Table** pop up. In this pop up, select `airline_otp_summary` and click on the **Finish** button, as shown in the following screenshot:

5. Next, you will see an **Import Data** dialog box; here you can change the actual query by clicking on the **Connection Properties**. If you suspect the data volume to be high, it is recommended that you use a limit clause to prevent your laptop from freezing. The following screenshot shows this pop up:

If you are editing the query, do verify the generated SQL. Excel, by default, will construct queries with table references such as `HIVE`.`otpdw`.`airline_otp_summary` which you will need to edit and remove the HIVE prefix to `otpdw`.`airline_otp_summary`.

6. Next, you have a choice to import the data as a simple table, PivotTable, or a PivotChart. Select **PivotChart**, and select the `flightyear` and `flightmonth` as rows, `airlinecarrier` as columns, and `averagedepdelay` as values. With a few clicks, you can quickly get a useful chart that shows you how each airline carrier performs using the average arrival delay as a measure and you can also compare it against its peers. Take a look at the following screenshot:

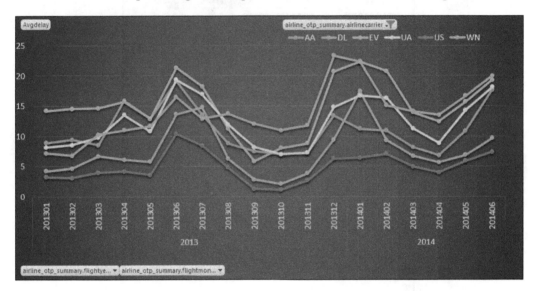

Let's take a moment to look at the chart and understand its key insights:

- Peak travel seasons in June and December are worst in delays
- US Airways (abbreviated **US**) is consistently better than other leading carriers
- Southwest (**WN**) and ExpressJet (**EV**) are the worst performing carriers

Let's understand how this works:

1. Microsoft Hive ODBC driver executes the HiveQL on the HDInsight cluster.
2. Hive converts this to a MapReduce job as per the query.
3. Results from the query are sent to the client PC where Excel is running.
4. Further, all analysis/charts will use data that is already imported to Excel.

Analysis using Excel Power Query

A key strategy of Microsoft's big data solution is the integration of **Business Intelligence (BI)** components with HDInsight. This is seen with the integration of Microsoft Power Query of Excel with data stored in the HDInsight cluster.

Let's take our airline on-time performance project; the summary analysis showed us that the flight from carrier EV in the month of June has high delays. If we want to get into further details, we can use Power Query in Excel to filter and search for the top flights delayed for that airline in that month.

Prerequisites

The prerequisites are as follows:

- Office 2013 Professional Plus, Office 365 Pro Plus, Excel 2013 Standalone, or Office 2010 Professional plus
- Operating systems that are supported are Windows 7, Windows 8, Windows Server 2008 R2, Windows Server 2012, Windows Vista (requires .NET 3.5 SP1), Windows Server 2008 (requires .NET 3.5 SP1), or Windows 8.1

Step 1 – installing the Microsoft Power Query for Excel

The first step is to download the Excel add-in from `http://www.microsoft.com/en-us/download/details.aspx?id=39379`.

Once you download the driver MSI file to your local machine, double-click on it to install the add-in.

 There are two versions of the installation package: 32 bit or 64 bit. You should install the version that matches your office installation.

Step 2 – importing Azure Blob storage data into Excel

To import data from an HDInsight cluster in Excel, you can import data associated with the cluster by performing the following steps:

1. Open Excel and create a new blank workbook.

2. Navigate to the new add-in **POWER QUERY | From Other Sources | From Microsoft Azure Blob Storage**, as shown in the following screenshot:

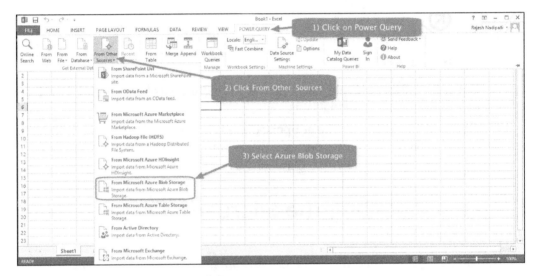

3. This will next prompt you for the Azure Blob Storage account name and account key associated with your HDInsight cluster. In our demo, it is **hdindstorage**.

4. Now, you will see the containers inside the Blob storage and the individual files. In our case, we are looking for the on-time performance file for the month of June 2013. Locate the file and then click on the **Binary** link on the left-hand side, as shown in the following screenshot. This allows us to search, sort, and apply Excel functions to this dataset.

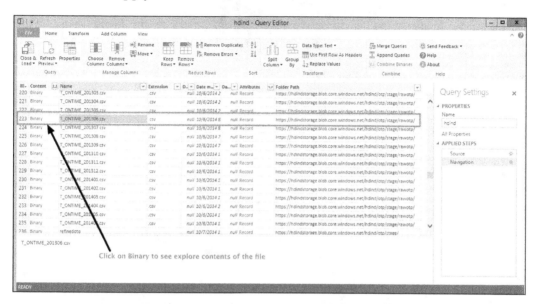

Step 3 – analyzing data using Excel

To analyze the data, filter the records where the airline carrier (**Column 7**) is EV and then sort it by the arrival delay (**Column 23**) descending.

This now give us a list of flights that were delayed significantly and caused the average arrival delay for flights from the EV carrier. Take a look at the following screenshot:

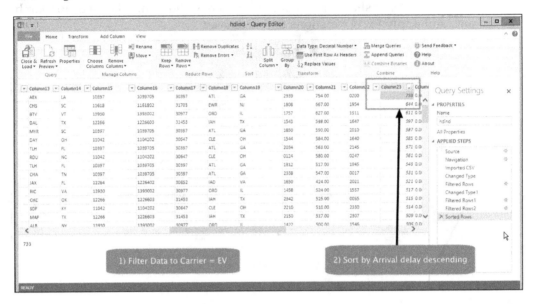

The data shows you certain flights that had over a 10-hour delay (over 600 minutes in **Column 23**). These outliers caused the average for this airline to go higher.

Let's understand how this works:

1. Microsoft Power Query plugin connects to Azure Blob storage.
2. Power Query plugin buffers a certain number of rows in Excel based on user criteria.
3. Results from the query are sent to the client PC where Excel is running.
4. Further, all analysis/charts will use data that is already imported to Excel.
5. This approach eliminates the need for a Hive table and directly reads from Azure Blob storage.

Other BI features in Excel

Excel has several other features and add-ins that make it a great tool for business intelligence. The following features are worth exploring for your analytics use cases.

For the features that are discussed in the following section, you might need to install additional software on top of Excel.

PowerPivot

The PowerPivot allows you to build a data model, calculate **key performance indicators (KPI)**, detect relationships, and visualize using charts or tables. The following screenshot shows you the **POWERPIVOT** menu:

Power View and Power Map

Power View reports allow a host of new visualizations of your KPIs, including a Map view where you can geographically report your results. This feature is under the **INSERT | Power View Reports** submenu, as shown in the following screenshot:

If your data has geographical information such as state, city, or latitude and longitude, you can visualize this information easily by a few clicks in Excel. Let's consider our sample project with airline on-time performance data for which the origin city code is a good candidate for the location and departure delay as a metric to visualize. To visualize this using Power Map, perform the steps mentioned in the following sections.

Step 1 – importing Azure Blob storage data into Excel

First, you can import Azure Blob Storage data into Excel, as described in the *Analysis using Excel Power Query* section.

Step 2 – launch map view

Next, click on the **INSERT** tab, click on **Map** icon, and then launch Power Map, as shown in the following screenshot. Power Map uses Bing to geocode the data based on its geographic properties.

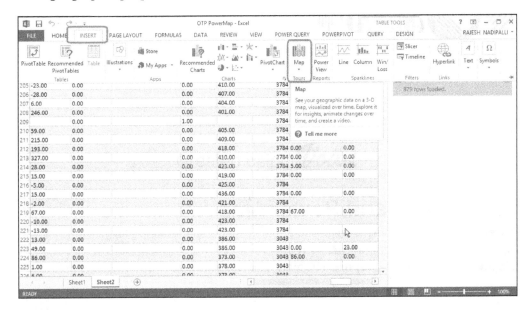

Step 3 – configure the map

Next, you will see the Power Map and the first screen of **Layer Pane** with the properties seen on the right-hand side. Let's change the **GEOGRAPHY** option to the Origin column and the Departure delay column as the metric to be displayed as a circle. Next, Power Map will plot the data and circles will appear on the map, as shown in the following screenshot. The size of the circle represents the number of flights from the city and the color represents the departure delay.

This approach can be used to visualize your data in geographic space and you can also see it change by time to gain new understandings.

Power BI Catalog

With Power BI Catalog feature, you can publish and share results with your coworkers in your organization. Additionally, you can clean, transform, and merge data from multiple sources.

Power BI Catalog is accessible under **POWER QUERY | My Data Catalog Queries**, as shown in the following screenshot:

For further information, refer to http://www.microsoft.com/en-us/powerBI/home/discover.aspx.

Ad hoc analysis using Hive

Historically, Hive was considered a good abstraction over MapReduce and for data extraction in batch mode. Hive was not considered as a good alternative for low latency queries; however, this is changing as you read this book. With Hive Version 13, you can run Hive over Apache Tez, which is faster and more efficient than the traditional MapReduce. This allows business users to explore and interact with data in HDInsight using BI tools such as Excel.

Other alternatives for analysis

The Hadoop ecosystem has several other specialized tools and projects for data analysis that might be applicable for your use case. I'll mention a few popular open source tools to be considered.

RHadoop

R is a language created for statisticians and has over 2 million users. RHadoop is a set of R packages that run on Hadoop, which are as follows:

- `rmr` package provides interface to MapReduce using R code
- `rhdfs` package provides interface to HDFS with R
- `rhbase` package is required if HBase is used
- `plyrmr` package has common data manipulation functions
- `ravro` package allows reading and writing to files in an `avro` format

With RHadoop, data scientists can explore the Data Lake, perform regression analysis to predict the future, identify customer segments and relationships to understand customer behavior, detect outliers for fraud detection, and perform other time series data mining.

Here are some useful links to get further details on RHadoop:

- `https://github.com/RevolutionAnalytics/RHadoop/wiki`
- `http://www.rstudio.com/products/rstudio/`

Apache Giraph

Apache Giraph allows graph processing using HDInsight cluster for large-scale graph analysis. Graphs model relationships between entities such as people, place, job, sale, and date. Graph processing allows you to understand the strength of these relations and has several use cases, which are as follows:

- Recommendations to a tourist on the shortest route between two cities by avoiding busy intersections

- Song recommendations based on users and their friends' history

- In our airline on-time performance project, the shortest route between two cities with less than two stops and 90 percent on-time performance.

For further information on how Facebook analyzed a trillion edges using Giraph, you can refer to https://www.facebook.com/notes/facebook-engineering/ scaling-apache-giraph-to-a-trillion-edges/10151617006153920.

Apache Mahout

Apache Mahout is a library of scalable machine learning algorithms implemented on top of Apache Hadoop and enables machines to learn without being explicitly programmed. Common use cases for Apache Mahout are as follows:

- **Collaborative filtering**: This algorithm mines user behaviors such as ratings, clicks, and purchases to provide recommendations to other users. Sites such as Amazon and Netflix use this approach.

- **Clustering**: This algorithm is used to group similar items together. For example, if a certain news article is trending, this algorithm can group news articles from public sources in one place to allow you to get a well-rounded review.

- **Categorization**: This algorithm is also referred to as classification. As documents are ingested to Data Lake, they are first tagged with one/more labels. Next, this algorithm can check the unclassified documents and tag them to the best category.

- **Frequent itemset**: This algorithm is used to analyze product placement and market basket analysis, for example, retailers realize that beer and diapers are generally purchased together so placing them close to each other helps their end customers.

The following are some reference links for Mahout:

- `http://blogs.technet.com/b/oliviaklose/archive/2014/04/14/`
  `mahout-for-dummies-2-step-by-step-mahout-and-hdinsight-`
  `interactive-style.aspx`
- `http://hortonworks.com/hadoop/mahout/`

Azure Machine Learning

Azure **Machine Learning** (**ML**) is an exciting addition to Azure's growing list of valuable cloud services and provides predictive analytics without the need of complex software and high-end computers.

Azure ML is very simple to use and does not require seasoned data scientists to mine data. Users can model using ML studio, which is launched using a web browser, and has a simple drag-and-drop designer. ML studio comes with a library of sample experiments using which you can create new experiments on your data stored in HDInsight.

Azure ML also allows data scientists to drop the existing R code directly into your workspace or author it directly in ML studio.

For further details on this preview feature, visit this website at `http://azure.`
`microsoft.com/en-us/services/machine-learning/`.

Summary

For any big data project to be successful, the key is to gain actionable information from the vast amount of data collected in the Data Lake. The familiar Microsoft Excel has several add-ins that make it a powerful business intelligence tool that allows one to model, analyze, report, and publish rich and interactive reports. PowerPivot, Power Query, Power BI, and Power Map work with data in HDInsight and other SQL stores.

Hadoop ecosystem has several additional tools such as RHadoop, Apache Giraph, and Apache Mahout. These allow data scientists and statisticians to detect patterns, predict future trends, and perform data mining.

In the next chapter, we will see some of the preview and new features of HDInsight that further enhance the Data Lake capabilities.

8

HDInsight 3.1 New Features

The latest HDInsight release is 3.1 and it has several new features. This chapter focuses on key new features that provide significant value to Data Lake customers. The topics covered in this chapter are as follows:

- **HBase**: A low latency NoSQL database
- **Storm**: A real-time stream based processing system
- **Tez**: A high-performance data processing framework

For a complete list of what's new in HDInsight 3.1, visit the webpage at `http://azure.microsoft.com/en-us/documentation/articles/hdinsight-component-versioning/`.

HBase

HBase is an open source NoSQL database built on Hadoop that provides random, real-time read/write access to Data Lake. HBase is modeled after Google's Bigtable project where data is organized in column-oriented format. The following are the key features of HBase:

- **Linear scalability**: HBase leverages the cluster and hence is scalable like Hadoop
- **Strictly consistent read and writes**: HBase is optimized for read performance. For writes, HBase seeks to maintain consistency
- **Automatic and configurable sharding**: HBase uses row keys to guide data sharding and distribute data throughout the cluster
- **Automatic recovery on failure**: HBase automatically recovers when a node fails and reassigns the region server that was handling the data to another node

- **Low latency queries**: HBase provides random and real-time access to data by utilizing memory, bloom filters, and efficient storage mechanisms

HBase positioning in Data Lake and use cases

Let's first understand where HBase fits in the overall Data Lake architecture. HDInsight and Hadoop serve as the long-term data stores and are great for "write once and read many times" type of applications, specifically batch processing. Hadoop is not suited for interactive web applications that require random read/write support. HBase was designed to address these shortcomings of Hadoop and provides a low latency database that can be used for applications. HBase in Azure leverages Azure Blob storage as the underlying storage. The following figure shows the HBase and HDInsight architecture:

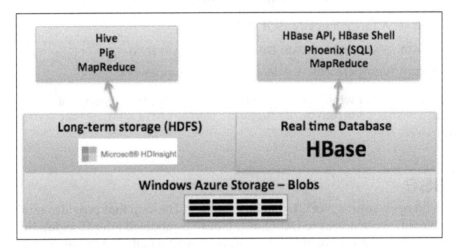

The following are some projects built on HBase:

- Facebook messaging platform switched from MySQL database to HBase for its scalability, performance and data consistency features. For further details, you can refer to `https://www.facebook.com/notes/facebook-engineering/the-underlying-technology-of-messages/454991608919`.

- Mendeley is a repository for research papers and is fully indexed and searchable. Researchers can read, annotate, and cite as they write new documents. The details about how they use HBase are available at `http://www.slideshare.net/danharvey/hbase-at-mendeley`.

- Veoh Networks uses HBase to store behavior data for 25 million unique visitors with real-time updates.

Provisioning HDInsight HBase cluster

This section describes how to provision an HBase cluster using the Azure portal. Perform the following steps to create a new HDInsight cluster with HBase enabled:

1. Login to Azure management portal and navigate to **NEW | DATA SERVICES | HDINSIGHT | HBASE**, as shown in the following screenshot:

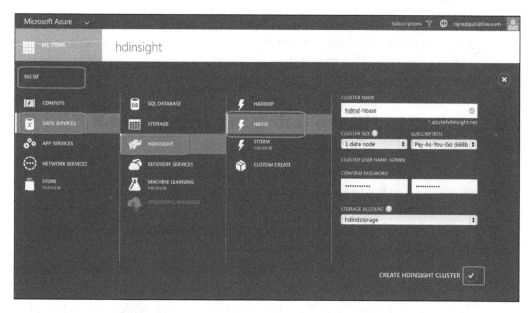

2. Enter the cluster name, cluster size, cluster password, and storage information.
3. Click on the check icon at the bottom-right corner and wait for the cluster to be provisioned.

Creating a sample HBase schema

To use HBase, you will be required to define a set of tables as well as the schemas for all the contained column families. The following section will show you how to create schemas for the airline on-time performance use case.

Designing the airline on-time performance table

An HBase table consists of a row and column like a traditional database table; however, the way it stores data is quite different. Each table must have a primary key and all queries to the table must use the primary key. Each row in the table can have any number of columns grouped together by column families.

Each column family is stored in a separate file and hence HBase is called a columnar database. HBase has a flexible schema that allows any number of columns to be added dynamically within the column families.

Let's take the example of our airline on-time performance data and see how it can be modeled for HBase data store. The row key will be a combination of `Date-Carrier-FlightNumber` making it easy to query. The following will be the column families:

- `Origindetails`: This will consist of the origin airport, origin state, departure time, and departure delay columns
- `Destinationdetails`: This will consist of the destination airport, destination state, arrival time, and arrival delay columns

Connecting to HBase using the HBase shell

The following are the steps to launch the HBase shell:

1. Enable remote desktop (RDP) connection to the new HDInsight cluster provisioned in the previous section using the **Configuration** tab from Azure management portal.

2. Next, connect to the head node using the RDP application and launch the Hadoop Command Line from the desktop.

3. Next, change the directory to the HBase `bin` directory; in the current cluster, it is `C:\apps\dist\hbase-0.98.0.2.1.6.0-2103-hadoop2\bin`.

4. Next, to launch the HBase shell, type in `hbase shell`, which will get you to the HBase prompt.

Creating an HBase table

The following commands will create a new table, `flight_hbase`, and describe the structure of the table:

```
hbase> create 'flight_hbase','Origindetails','Destinationdetails'

hbase> describe 'flight_hbase'
```

The following screenshot shows the results of the `describe` command:

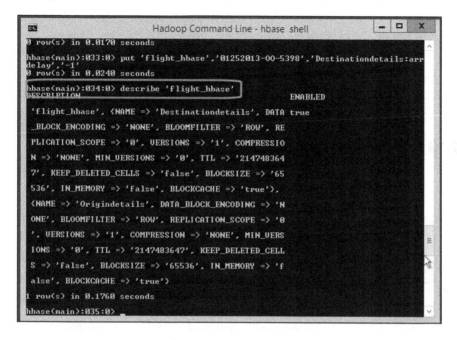

Loading data to the HBase table

The following commands will insert records to the `flight_hbase` table:

```
put 'flight_hbase','01272013-UA-1499','Origindetails:originairportabr','I
AH'
put 'flight_hbase','01272013-UA-1499','Origindetails:originstateabr','TX'
put 'flight_hbase','01272013-UA-1499','Origindetails:deptime','1858'
put 'flight_hbase','01272013-UA-1499','Origindetails:depdelay','-3'
put 'flight_hbase','01272013-UA-1499','Destinationdetails:destairportabr'
,'MSP'
put 'flight_hbase','01272013-UA-1499','Destinationdetails:deststateabr','
MN'
put 'flight_hbase','01272013-UA-1499','Destinationdetails:arrtime','132'
put 'flight_hbase','01272013-UA-1499','Destinationdetails:arrdelay','-27'
```

Querying data from the HBase table

To query the table data, the HBase shell has two options: `scan` that gets all the records and `get` that can be used to query a specific row based on the row key. The following are the commands:

```
scan 'flight_hbase'
get  'flight_hbase', '01272013-UA-1499'
```

HBase additional information

In this section about HBase, we reviewed how to provision an HDInsight HBase cluster, create a table, insert data, and retrieve data from HBase using HBase shell. To get additional information about HDInsight and HBase, review the web page at `http://azure.microsoft.com/en-us/documentation/articles/hdinsight-hbase-overview/`.

Storm

Apache Storm is a scalable, fault-tolerant, distributed, real-time computation system. Storm makes it easy to reliably process streams of data. Storm has many use cases: real-time analytics, online machine learning, continuous computation, ETL, and others. Storm can process over 1 million tuples per second per node. The following are the key features of Storm:

- Real-time computation
- Guarantees data will be processed
- Scalable
- Fault tolerant

 At the time this book was authored, Storm is a preview feature in Azure HDInsight.

Storm positioning in Data Lake

Hadoop and MapReduce provide a great batch processing capability. HBase provides the low latency store. Storm provides low latency transformation so that real-time processing can be performed on the raw data.

Let's consider our airline on-time performance use case. In the previous chapters, we saw how to ingest, transform, and analyze historical data using batch processing. With Storm, we can now process real-time feeds and analyze both historical and real time at the same time. The following figure shows the data flow from source to analysis:

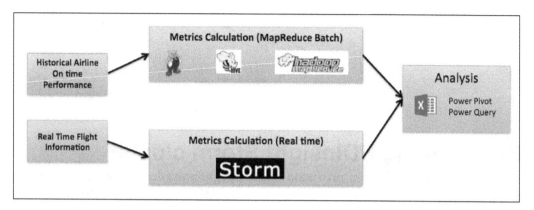

Storm key concepts

A Storm cluster is similar to a Hadoop cluster and has a master and several worker nodes. In a Storm cluster, "topologies" run similar to "MapReduce" that runs on a Hadoop cluster. One key difference is that a MapReduce job does eventually finish but a Storm topology is always running and processing messages.

The master/head node of Storm is called **Nimbus** and is responsible for distributing code around the various worker nodes, which is similar to YARN ResourceManager. HDInsight provides two Nimbus nodes so that there is no single point of failure for the Storm cluster. Each worker node runs a supervisor that is responsible for starting worker processes on the node.

A topology is a graph of computation where each node contains the processing logic and the links between nodes, which dictate how data is transferred between the nodes. A topology is distributed across several worker processes and will continue to run unless you stop it.

To build a topology, we need to start with a stream, which is an unbounded sequence of tuples. For example, a stream of Twitter feeds. A **spout** is a source of streams. For example, a spout might connect to Twitter API and emit a stream of tweets. A bolt can consume a number of input streams, process, and emit new streams.

This network of spouts and bolts are packaged into a topology. The following figure shows a sample topology:

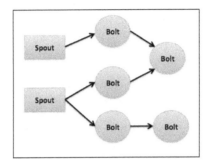

Provisioning HDInsight Storm cluster

This section describes how to provision an HDInsight Storm cluster using Azure portal. Perform the following steps to create a new HDInsight cluster with Storm:

1. Login to Azure management portal and navigate to **NEW | DATA SERVICES | HDINSIGHT | STORM**, as shown in the following screenshot:

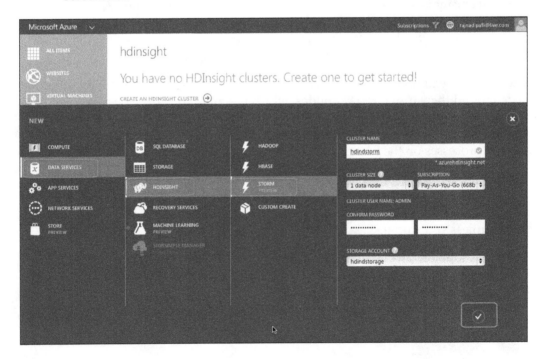

2. Enter the cluster name, cluster size, cluster password, and storage information.

3. Click on the check icon at the bottom-right corner and wait for the cluster to be provisioned.

Running a sample Storm topology

In this section, we will review how to run a sample Storm topology that is preinstalled with HDInsight.

Connecting to Storm using Storm shell

The following are the steps to launch the Storm shell:

1. Enable remote desktop (RDP) connection to the new HDInsight cluster provisioned in the previous section using the **Configuration** tab from Azure management portal.

2. Next, connect to the head node using the RDP application and launch the Hadoop Command Line from the desktop.

3. Click on the **Storm Command Line** shortcut from the desktop.

4. Navigate to the `bin` directory and then you can list the commands by typing the word `storm` without any parameters. The following is a screenshot of the various options seen after you type this command:

Running the Storm Wordcount topology

HDInsight comes packaged with a working example of Storm, which is the basic Wordcount example. To start this Storm topology, enter the following commands from the Storm Command Line.

```
C:\apps\dist\storm-0.9.1.2.1.6.0-2013\bin>storm jar ..\contrib\storm-
starter\storm-starter-0.9.1.2.1.6.0-2103-jar-with-dependencies.jar storm.
starter.WordCountTopology wordcount
```

Once this topology starts, there is no message on the command line as it is running in the background.

Monitoring status of the Wordcount topology

For the sample Wordcount topology that we started in the previous step, HDInsight provides a web page to show the status. Perform the following steps to get to the logs of the topology:

1. From the remote desktop, double-click on the **Storm UI** shortcut provided on the desktop; this will bring up the Storm UI main dashboard. Next, under the **Topology summary** section, click on the **wordcount** link, which will show the details of that specific topology:

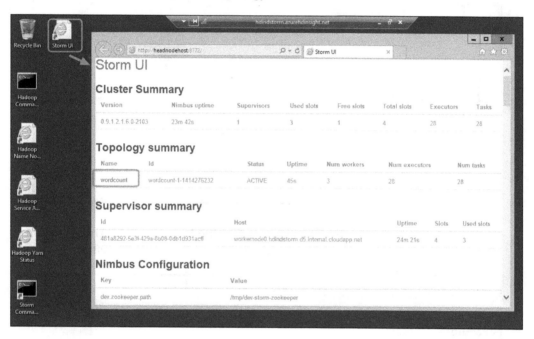

2. Next, under the **Spouts (All time)** section, click on the **spout** link, which will show the details of that specific spout, as shown in the following screenshot:

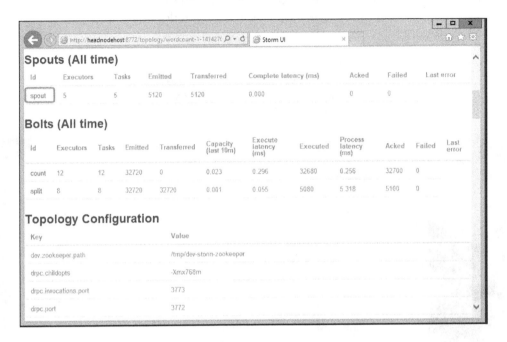

3. Next, from the Spout details page, scroll to the **Executors (All time)** section and click on one of the ports, as shown in the following screenshot:

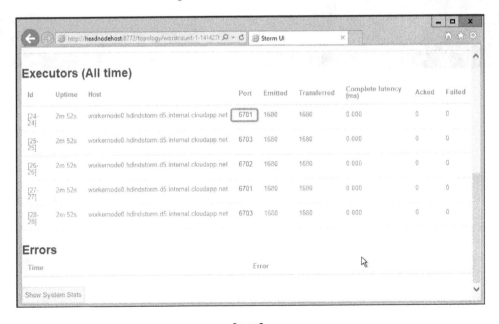

4. After you click on the executor link, you will see the log information from the spout. In this Wordcount sample, the spouts emits sentences such as "snow white and the seven dwarfs", which are then split into words by a bolt, and then counted by another bolt. These sentences will keep changing based on what the spout emits. The following is a screenshot of the log:

Additional information on Storm

Storm can consume data from services such as Azure Service Bus queues and Event Hubs. Additionally, it can also integrate with Apache Kafka, which is a high-throughput distributed messaging system. For further information on Storm and Kafka, you can visit the following websites:

- `http://kafka.apache.org/`

- `http://azure.microsoft.com/en-us/documentation/articles/hdinsight-storm-overview/`

- `http://azure.microsoft.com/en-us/documentation/articles/hdinsight-storm-sensor-data-analysis/`

- `http://azure.microsoft.com/en-us/documentation/articles/hdinsight-hadoop-storm-scpdotnet-csharp-develop-streaming-data-processing-application/`

Apache Tez

Apache Tez is an extensible framework for YARN-based high-performance data processing applications. Projects such as Hive and Pig can leverage this framework for improved performance and faster response times and they can be used for interactive needs.

HDInsight 3.1 is capable of running Hive queries using Tez, which provides substantial performance improvements over MapReduce. By default, Tez is not enabled for Hive and can be enabled, as shown in the following code snippet:

```
set hive.execution_engine=tez;

select flightyear, flightquarter, flightmonth ,
    regexp_replace(uniquecarrier,"\"","") as airlinecarrier,
avg(depdelay) as avgdepdelay

from airline_otp_refined

group by flightyear, flightquarter, flightmonth ,

regexp_replace(uniquecarrier,"\"","");
```

Summary

The Hadoop ecosystem and HDInsight platform are constantly evolving and new components are being added with every release that enable new use cases and improved experience for data consumers. In this chapter, we reviewed HBase, Storm, and Tez. HBase provides a low latency database that currently powers applications such as Facebook messaging. Storm provides real-time data processing capabilities and complements the batch processing with MapReduce. Tez is the next generation MapReduce-like framework built on top of YARN projects such as Hive and Pig can be leveraged for improved performance.

In the next chapter, we will review the tips and architectural considerations for starting a new Data Lake initiative.

9

Strategy for a Successful Data Lake Implementation

The Data Lake vision and promise is to transform the vast amount of big data into real insights that help drive fact-based decisions. We are now witnessing this dream being realized in several enterprises across multiple industries such as fashion, food, retail, banks, and others. While there are a few success stories, there are a significant number of organizations that have the new platform stuck in development or proof of concept stage and are unable to move to production.

In this chapter, I will share the approaches to ensure a successful big data project. The topics covered in this chapter are as follows:

- Challenges on building a production Data Lake
- The success path for a sustainable production Data Lake
- Architectural considerations
- Online resources

Challenges on building a production Data Lake

Most organizations start with a short **proof of concept** (**POC**) that demonstrates the value of big data and the Hadoop ecosystem. These are primarily executed from a research perspective with specific datasets and goals and are generally successful.

After the **proof of technology** (POT) readout is when management has the following key questions that block further progress:

- Do we have the development skills to handle this technology on a large scale?
- How do we integrate this Hadoop Data Lake with current systems?
- How do we secure data in Hadoop and meet compliance requirements?
- Can the current operations team manage this in production?

These are tough questions and require people, process, and technology to transition so that the organization can leap forward to a modern Data Lake architecture. In the next section, we will review a few key steps for a successful Data Lake implementation.

The success path for a production Data Lake

For a successful production Data Lake transition, there are three key steps:

- Identify the big data problem
- Conduct a successful proof of technology
- Form a Data Lake Center of Excellence

Let's review each of these steps in detail.

Identifying the big data problem

A big data solution should not be considered as a hammer looking for a nail but a solution for a real business problem. The first step for a Data Lake journey is to evaluate your current state architecture and business needs to see whether there is a real big data problem. It is possible that some of your current systems are better suited for handling your business requirements than a new Data Lake.

To give you some ideas, the following are the top use cases of a Hadoop-based Data Lake and might be relevant to your organization:

- **ETL offload**: Hadoop MapReduce provides a low cost alternative for the traditional batch-oriented extract-transform-load. Offloading this to Hadoop will free up your data warehouse to perform high-value functions such as analytics and reporting.

- **Active data archival**: Data archival solutions for a typical relational database have been the magnetic tapes that are typically stored offsite and takes days to restore. With a Data Lake based on HDFS, data can be archived onto low cost commodity hardware and can always be available for queries and hence "active archive".

- **Log analytics**: A modern Data Lake based on Hadoop is well-suited for analyzing server logs that are useful to manage applications and to detect security breaches.

- **Advanced analytics**: A Data Lake built on top of Hadoop empowers data scientists to explore and create insights straight from unstructured data without the need for complex and expensive data preparation. This unprecedented flexibility opens new possibilities for agile analytics.

While these are some common patterns, there might be several other use cases that pertain to your business, which current systems are unable to keep up with, such as the data volume or business demand, and they could be candidates for the modern Data Lake. It is also advisable to have a priority of your business use cases based on impact and return on investment. Ensure that you capture and document executive and business buy-in for future traceability.

For example, the multinational company GE conducted a study on the business value of the Industrial Internet and found that 1 percent reduction in system inefficiencies in healthcare will translate to $63 billion of savings over a 15-year period. This study built a great business case for GE management to invest in big data infrastructure and initiatives. The following figure shows the potential business value of the investment:

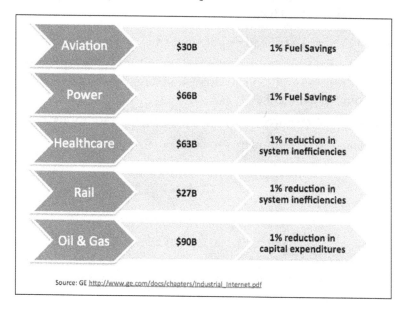

Proof of technology for Data Lake

After you have identified a set of use cases that demonstrate potential business value, the next step is to conduct a short **proof of technology (POT)** with a limited set of those use cases. This should be time bound with specific success criteria. The following should be in your proof of technology plan:

- **POT objectives**: This should include the dataset for POT, sample data, desired aggregates, integrations, and success criteria
- **Infrastructure considerations**: This should include the factors such as will this architecture scale, be available, meet the SLAs as data grows, and will it be manageable?
- **Timeline and Resources**: This should have the start and end dates with resources identified
- **POT readout**: POT should have a closure date with a readout to the stakeholders

A successful POT will provide management support to proceed with a larger production scale rollout.

Form a Data Lake Center of Excellence

Organizations should not stop at a successful POT. If the management sees value in the Data Lake architecture, then they should next set up a **Center of Excellence (COE)**. A new core team should be formed that champions the technology, process, and governance of the Data Lake. The following are the benefits of building such a COE:

- A unified Data Lake instead of potential silos based on business units resulting in lower total cost of ownership and avoiding redundancy
- Consistent process and tools for ingestion, organization, and extraction to and from the Data Lake
- Talented pool of resources for addressing big data solutions
- Operational and development efficiencies

The following figure shows the four key subteams required to form a Data Lake COE:

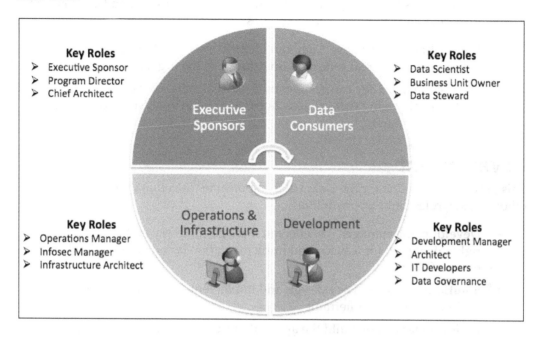

Let's review the responsibilities for each of the quarters of the preceding COE:

Executive sponsors

This group is the key for keeping the Data Lake initiative alive and consists of the following roles and responsibilities:

- **Visionary director/vice president**: This person believes in big data and is committed by funding the initiative.

- **Program director**: This person overlooks all the projects on boarding and consuming Data Lake.

- **Chief technology architect**: This person is responsible for the overall Data Lake architecture design and implementation that supports business strategy. He/she is also responsible for approving tools, technology, and frameworks, which form the foundation of a Data Lake.

Data Lake consumers

This group identifies the business problems that are appropriate for a Data Lake and has the following key roles and responsibilities:

- **Line of business owners**: They can identify use cases that are fit for the Data Lake and provide real return on investment to the organization

- **Data scientists**: They can demonstrate the real value of the information in the Data Lake using pattern detections, regression analysis, and other data mining techniques

Development

This group is the lifeline for the Data Lake responsible for actual delivery and has the following key roles and responsibilities:

- **Development manager**: This person manages delivery and builds the right talent pool for a successful implementation based on direction from the chief architect

- **Solution architects**: They design and implement solutions for specific projects within the timeframe

- **IT developers**: They build the applications using a common framework and tools

- **Data governance team**: This team defines and overlooks policies to ensure data quality and integrity of the Data Lake

Operations and infrastructure

This group ensures that the lights are always on for the Data Lake and has the following key roles and responsibilities:

- **Operations manager**: This person is responsible for the Data Lake availability, including the core platform and the applications built on top of it by meeting the business **service level agreements (SLA)**

- **Information security (Infosec) manager**: This person is responsible for protecting the organization's assets and ensures that the right folks have access to the right data

- **Infrastructure architect**: This person is responsible for the hardware and software strategy to keep up with the SLA and growth demands for a Data Lake

An organization that plans, forms, and integrates these various teams will reap the benefits for a successful Data Lake program that can scale to the business needs.

Architectural considerations

A modern Data Lake based on Hadoop is now mainstream technology and is used in several public sectors and enterprises; however, the ecosystem is still evolving and new tools and projects are released every quarter. In the next few sections, I will highlight the key architectural considerations to ensure that your Data Lake is well-planned and extensible for years to come.

Extensible and modular

In *Chapter 2, Enterprise Data Lake using HDInsight*, we looked into the reference architecture for the next generation Data Lake, as shown in the following figure. Use this architecture to design and build reusable components and well-defined interfaces between each layer, which allows a pluggable model. Let's take an example for the processing layer if you start with Pig as your ELT and later decide to switch to a newer technology such as Spark; this change will be contained within the **Processing** layer of the stack and will not impact the other layers as long as the interface agreements between the layers are maintained.

The following are the other considerations while building components of the stack:

- **Use of frameworks**: As far as possible, use an existing framework instead of a custom-built framework, as this helps with long-term maintenance of the component.

- **Reusable components**: Every component that is designed should be implemented with a configuration that will improve the chances for reusability.

- **Scalable**: HDInsight and Hadoop are meant to scale and hence any application that is built for the Data Lake should be designed to scale and should be planned to be distributed.

- **Support agile development**: Agile-based development is the preferred approach for most organizations. This model allows natural evolution of components with features that get added incrementally at each sprint with an engaged end user, thereby improving the chance of adoption.

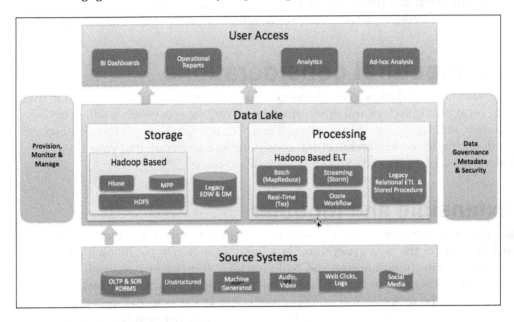

Metadata-driven solution

For each component, a metadata-driven solution will help development and streamline operations. The following are a few examples of how a metadata-driven design will help the Data Lake development and operations:

- For all data sources, consider a metadata of database names, table names, file patterns, and frequency of ingestion. This can be used to build an automated registration process for onboarding new providers and also help the operations team prepare to troubleshoot ingestion issues.

- For all workflows that need to transform data in the Data Lake, consider a listing of workflows, workflow type batch or streaming, script location (MapReduce/Hive/Pig), parameters, scheduling, and logging. This will help developers manage and reuse code wherever applicable.

- For all scheduled extracts from the Data Lake, consider a metadata repository that has all the target system information such as FTP site/database name, credential if required, frequency, and contact information. This can be used to automate extraction processes and notify owners in case of an outage or impact to their process.

Integration strategy

Plan and build a good integration strategy for both upstream and downstream systems. Typical implementations involve an edge node that is dedicated for receiving files and ingests to HDInsight. For sending data out of HDInsight, you can set up scheduled workflows to export data out of the cluster to the external system or have the downstream system query HDFS via Hive/Pig.

Security

Hadoop has POSIX style filesystem security with three roles: users, groups, and others, and read/write/execute for each role. This allows the basic filesystem security that can be used to manage access by functional users defined per application. Hadoop does integrate with Kerberos for network-based authentication. If your data has **personal identifiable information (PII)**, you can consider masking and/or tokenization to ensure that the information is protected.

Online resources

HDInsight has several resources available online for both beginners and advanced users. Here are some useful websites and blogs that will help you in building a modern Data Lake based on HDInsight:

URL	Description
`http://azure.microsoft.com/en-us/documentation/articles/hdinsight-learn-map/`	This is an HDInsight documentation with learning map-based on the following categories: • Managing cluster • Uploading data • Developing and running jobs • Real-world scenarios • Latest release notes
`http://azure.microsoft.com/en-us/documentation/services/hdinsight/`	This is an HDInsight documentation with tutorials, videos, forums, and downloads
`http://feedback.azure.com/forums/217335-hdinsight`	This website has feedback from customers/developers and you can vote for topics to influence the product roadmap
`http://anindita9.wordpress.com/`	Anindita Basak has regular updates on features and use cases on big data, machine learning, and analytics on Azure

URL	Description
`https://www.facebook.com/ MicrosoftBigData`	This is a Facebook account that provides the latest updates on HDInsight
`http://blogs.msdn.com/b/ cindygross/`	This is Cindy Gross' blog, which has several examples on using HDInsight and BI
`https://github.com/Azure/ azure-content`	This is a repository of sample code from various contributors on Azure, which you can further filter to articles related to HDInsight
`http://hortonworks.com/hdp/`	This is the Hortonworks Data Platform, which is the underlying platform for HDInsight and it has great information for building a modern data architecture

Summary

To gain a competitive edge over their peers, organizations are looking for technologies such as HDInsight to provide breakthrough insights from the vast amount of structured and unstructured data. While the promise and value of a modern Data Lake is clear, the journey requires proper planning of people, process, and technology. A key success factor is to build a Big Data Center of Excellence that can champion the cause and execute with skilled resource delivering solutions for real business problems.

These are exciting times for all of us working with big data and we have the opportunity to make a big difference leveraging the next generation Data Lake platform. Good luck on your journey!

Index

HBase
about 129, 134
connecting, with HBase shell 132
features 129, 130
HDInsight HBase cluster, provisioning 131
positioning, in Data Lake 130
projects 130
URL 130, 134
use cases 130
HBase shell
launching 132
HBase table
creating 132
data, loading 133
data, querying 134
HCatalog
about 94
benefits 89
HCatalog Command Line used, for creating
tables 90-92
used, for managing file metadata 88, 89
HCatalog Command Line
used, for creating tables 90-92
HCatalog metastore
persisting, in SQL database 94
HDFS
basic commands 15
Data Lake, organizing in 87, 88
file, reading from 15
file, writing to 14
overview 14
transferring to 80
HDInsight
Apache Hive, starting 97
Apache Pig, starting 99
distribution, key differentiators 19
documentation , URL 151
MapReduce, executing 102
overview 19
URL 134
HDInsight cluster
monthly pricing, estimating for 40
provisioning 42-47
provisioning, Azure PowerShell used 45
topology 44

HDInsight Emulator
about 19, 21
for development 55
installation verification 56
installing 56
URL, for installing 56
using 56
HDInsight HBase cluster
provisioning 131
HDInsight management dashboard
about 48
CONFIGURATION tab 49, 50
DASHBOARD page 48
MONITOR tab 49
HDInsight Storm cluster
provisioning 136
Hive ODBC Data Source
creating 113-115
Hortonworks Data Platform (HDP) 20, 22

I

IBM BigInsights
URL 19
installation, HDInsight Emulator
about 56
verification 56
**installation, Microsoft Hive ODBC
driver 112**
installation, Microsoft Power Query
for Excel 119

J

journal nodes 15

K

Kafka
URL 141
key metadata, Data Lake
file inventory 32
structural metadata 32
user-defined information 32
key performance indicators (KPI) 26, 123
Knox (Apache Knox) 21

L

legacy EDW and DM 30
legacy ETL 30
Locally Redundant storage (LRS) 41
logging, storage account configuration 69

M

mapper code, MapReduce 101
MapR
  URL 19
MapReduce
  about 11, 100
  driver code 102
  executing, on HDInsight 102
  mapper code 101
  reducer code 101
  URL 100
master nodes
  about 12
  functions 13
Microsoft Azure HDInsight Service 21
Microsoft HDInsight
  URL 19
Microsoft Hive ODBC driver
  installing 112
  URL, for downloading 112
Microsoft Power Query
  installing, for Excel 119
monitoring, storage account
    configuration 69
MONITOR tab, HDInsight management
    dashboard 49

N

NameNode 13
next generation Hadoop-based Enterprise
    data architecture
  about 27
  Data Lake 29
  source systems 29
  user access 30
NodeManager
  containers 16
Nutch Distributed Filesystem (NDFS) 10

O

online transactional processing (OLTP) 19
on-time performance (OTP) 93
Oozie 110
operational reports 26
OTP project transformations
  about 104
  data cleaning, Apache Pig used 105
  Hive script, executing 109
  Pig script, executing 106
  results, reviewing 109
  steps 104

P

pain points, EDW
  about 27
  cost 27
  scale 27
  timeliness 27
  unstructured data 27
personal identifiable information (PII) 151
Platform as a Service (PaaS) 19
plyrmr package 126
Power BI Catalog
  about 125
  URL 125
Power Map 123
PowerPivot 123
Power View 123
processing mechanisms, Data Lake
  Hadoop Batch (MapReduce) 30
  Hadoop Oozie workflows 30
  Hadoop Real time (Tez) 30
  Hadoop Streaming (Storm) 30
  legacy ETL 30
processing mechanisms, EDW
  ETL 25
  SQL-based stored procedures 25
proof of technology (POT), Data Lake
  about 146
  infrastructure considerations 146
  objectives 146
  readout 146
  timeline and resources 146

R

ravro package 126
Read Access Geo-Redundant storage
    (RA-GRS) 41
reducer code, MapReduce 101
remote desktop
  used, for exploring cluster 51
replication, storage account
    configuration 69
ResourceManager
  components 16
RHadoop
  about 126
  reference links 126
rhbase package 126
rhdfs package 126
rmr package 126

S

sample HBase schema
  airline on-time performance table,
    creating 131
  connecting, with HBase shell 132
  data, loading to HBase table 133
  data, querying from HBase table 134
  HBase table, creating 132
sample MapReduce
  running 52-54
sample Storm topology
  connecting, with Storm shell 137
  running 137
  Wordcount topology, running 138
  Wordcount topology status,
    monitoring 139
Secondary NameNode 13
solution, based on HDInsight
  about 34
  benefits 36
  processing 36
  source systems 35
  storage 35
  user access 36
source systems, EDW architecture
  about 24
  OLTP databases 24

XML and text files 24
Spark 110
spout 135
SQL database
  HCatalog metastore, persisting 94
Sqoop
  benefits 85
  modes 86
  operation modes, Sqoop export 86
  operation modes, Sqoop import 86
  used, for importing data 86, 87
  used, for transferring data 85
Sqoop User Guide
  URL 87
storage access keys 82
storage account
  registering 83
storage container
  creating 46
storage tools 82
Storm
  about 129, 134
  features 134
  HDInsight Storm cluster, provisioning 136
  key concepts 135
  positioning, in Data Lake 134
  references 141
  URL 141
Storm shell
  launching 137
Storm Wordcount topology
  running 138
  status, monitoring 139-141

T

Tez (Apache Tez) 20
tools, Hadoop ecosystem
  Ambari 34
  Excel 34
  Flume 33
  HCatalog 33
  Hive 34
  Mahout 34
  Oozie 33
  Pig 33

Thank you for buying
HDInsight Essentials
Second Edition

About Packt Publishing

Packt, pronounced 'packed', published its first book, *Mastering phpMyAdmin for Effective MySQL Management*, in April 2004, and subsequently continued to specialize in publishing highly focused books on specific technologies and solutions.

Our books and publications share the experiences of your fellow IT professionals in adapting and customizing today's systems, applications, and frameworks. Our solution-based books give you the knowledge and power to customize the software and technologies you're using to get the job done. Packt books are more specific and less general than the IT books you have seen in the past. Our unique business model allows us to bring you more focused information, giving you more of what you need to know, and less of what you don't.

Packt is a modern yet unique publishing company that focuses on producing quality, cutting-edge books for communities of developers, administrators, and newbies alike. For more information, please visit our website at www.packtpub.com.

About Packt Enterprise

In 2010, Packt launched two new brands, Packt Enterprise and Packt Open Source, in order to continue its focus on specialization. This book is part of the Packt Enterprise brand, home to books published on enterprise software – software created by major vendors, including (but not limited to) IBM, Microsoft, and Oracle, often for use in other corporations. Its titles will offer information relevant to a range of users of this software, including administrators, developers, architects, and end users.

Writing for Packt

We welcome all inquiries from people who are interested in authoring. Book proposals should be sent to author@packtpub.com. If your book idea is still at an early stage and you would like to discuss it first before writing a formal book proposal, then please contact us; one of our commissioning editors will get in touch with you.

We're not just looking for published authors; if you have strong technical skills but no writing experience, our experienced editors can help you develop a writing career, or simply get some additional reward for your expertise.

HDInsight Essentials

ISBN: 978-1-84969-536-7   Paperback: 122 pages

Tap your unstructured Big Data and empower your business using the Hadoop distribution from Windows

1. Architect a Hadoop solution with a modular design for data collection, distributed processing, analysis, and reporting.

2. Build a multinode Hadoop cluster on Windows servers.

3. Establish a Big Data solution using HDInsight with open source software, and provide useful Excel reports.

Big Data Analytics with R and Hadoop

ISBN: 978-1-78216-328-2   Paperback: 238 pages

Set up an integrated infrastructure of R and Hadoop to turn your data analytics into Big Data analytics

1. Write Hadoop MapReduce within R.

2. Learn data analytics with R and the Hadoop platform.

3. Handle HDFS data within R.

4. Understand Hadoop streaming with R.

Please check **www.PacktPub.com** for information on our titles

Hadoop MapReduce Cookbook

ISBN: 978-1-84951-728-7   Paperback: 300 pages

Recipes for analyzing large and complex datasets with Hadoop MapReduce

1. Learn to process large and complex data sets, starting simply, then diving in deep.

2. Solve complex big data problems such as classifications, finding relationships, online marketing, and recommendations.

3. More than 50 Hadoop MapReduce recipes, presented in a simple and straightforward manner, with step-by-step instructions and real-world examples.

Hadoop Operations and Cluster Management Cookbook

ISBN: 978-1-78216-516-3   Paperback: 368 pages

Over 60 recipes showing you how to design, configure, manage, monitor, and tune a Hadoop cluster

1. Hands-on recipes to configure a Hadoop cluster from bare metal hardware nodes.

2. Practical and in depth explanation of cluster management commands.

3. Easy-to-understand recipes for securing and monitoring a Hadoop cluster, and design considerations.

4. Recipes showing you how to tune the performance of a Hadoop cluster.

Please check **www.PacktPub.com** for information on our titles

www.ingramcontent.com/pod-product-compliance
Lightning Source LLC
Chambersburg PA
CBHW060135060326
40690CB00018B/3888